Simon Parke was a priest in the Church of England for twenty years. He then worked for three years in a supermarket and is now a freelance author. He has been writing professionally for twenty-five years, producing scripts for TV and radio, including for *Spitting Image* and Simon Mayo. His most recent books are *The Beautiful Life* and *The Enneagram: a private session with the world's greatest psychologist*. Simon runs and leads retreats, meets with people looking for a new way in their life, and follows the beautiful game. For more information, please see www.simonparke.com.

SHELF LIFE

How I found the meaning of life
stacking supermarket shelves

Simon Parke

RIDER

LONDON · SYDNEY · AUCKLAND · JOHANNESBURG

1 3 5 7 9 10 8 6 4 2

Published in 2009 by Rider, an imprint of Ebury Publishing
A Random House Group Company

The Random House Group Limited Reg. No. 954009

Addresses for companies within
The Penguin Random House Group can be found at:
global.penguinrandomhouse.com

A CIP catalogue record for this book is available from the British Library

The Random House Group Limited supports The Forest Stewardship
Council (FSC), the leading international forest certification organisation.
All our titles that are printed on Greenpeace approved FSC certified paper
carry the FSC logo.
Our paper procurement policy can be found at
www.rbooks.co.uk/environment

Designed and typeset by Jerry Goldie Graphic Design
Printed and bound in Great Britain by Clays Ltd, Elcograf S.p.A.

ISBN 9781846041563

Copies are available at special rates for bulk orders. Contact the sales development team on
020 7840 8487 for more information

To buy books by your favourite authors and register for offers visit
www.rbooks.co.uk

To Paul Carter —
a good man in the newspaper trade;
all kindness, soul and skill.

CONTENTS

Acknowledgements

My thanks to:
The *Daily Mail* — the first to take a risk on
these supermarket diaries.

All at Rider and in particular my editor Judith Kendra —
a gracious and perceptive handler of this
rough-edged material.

My agent and friend Richard Addis — who writes too well
to be wasting his time on my efforts.

Sapphy, Garry, Caspar, Winston, Brian, Mohammed, Faith,
Rosemary, Toad, Stav, Lottie, Pinocchio, Sonny, Bryn, Manik,
Kong — and all other colleagues on shelf and till.

Those were the days, my friends, and I'm grateful.
'Till death us do part!' as we supermarket workers say...

1.

A Slight Change of Direction

In which a priest becomes an ex-priest and Winston makes plans to leave — again. Michael the lorry driver mucks in; Bryn eyes up Faith; it's tales of the unexpected in a bedroom at 2.00 am — and caffeine makes all things well.

People say that I have changed direction, though I'm not sure this is true. Certainly I was a priest in the Church of England for twenty years, before becoming a supermarket worker. But really, what's the difference? Roles may change, but unless we do, things are pretty much the same. We take ourselves wherever we go, and attract or repel life accordingly.

Take Winston, who is standing to my left on the till, as we face the lunchtime rush. He tells me he once had an ambition to be rich and married by thirty-three. He is now forty, single and poor, so on the face of it, things have not worked out as planned. He's not a happy man, and imagines a change of job will help: 'I need a change of direction, Simon,' he says. 'A big change of direction.'

'What will you do?'

'I don't know, but whatever it is, it will be a whole lot better than this. This is not what I want to be doing.'

But he isn't unhappy because of the job. He's not even unhappy because he's poor or single, for he had a propensity for unhappiness way before that. He's unhappy because he's Winston; or a version of Winston at least. No external change of direction would make any difference to the congealed rage he keeps sealed inside.

No, I didn't expect to be a shelf-filler at the age of fifty; or standing on the till, watched by suspicious customer eyes. I suppose I'd imagined I'd be a priest for life – burying, marrying, baptising. And organising the increasingly big annual parish pantomime. Fantastic! I'd even preached at St Paul's Cathedral a couple of times, and for a short while had aspirations to be a bishop. Imagine it. A pointy hat and robes dripping with gold! How grand it all might have been. Instead, I am rear-ranging organic carrots, scraping the scum off the banana stand and date-rotating the fruit salads, because after twenty years, I knew the adventure was over. It was time to leave the insti-tutional Church.

Perhaps from the outside it looked like a choice. To many, it was perhaps a shocking choice, and a dereliction of duty. There was anger at my decision – anger from those who need you to be something for them. The roles we play can give other people's lives a semblance of order, and when roles change, or are abandoned, it can be unsettling for the fragile; those who struggle to manage their inner chaos. With no inner pillars of their own, they need others to be strong pillars for them. Such folk are not helped by resign-ing priests: 'Once a priest, always a priest surely?'

'Has he lost his faith?'

'Makes you wonder, doesn't it?'

'Such a waste.'

'And rather sad, don't you think?'

'I remember the time when a vocation was a vocation.'

'Unhappy with his job? In my day, you just got on with it.'

From the inside, however, it was no choice at all. When your home is on fire, you leave. I wouldn't call that a choice. It is something you simply do. And so I simply did – I left the church, my security, my home and my keeper – and took up stacking shelves in a supermarket, because, like Winston, I couldn't find anything else either. It was all simply mad – but happy also. The simple mind knows no obstacles.

There are others here who might wish for themselves another direction. Take our lorry driver, Michael. Lorry drivers are honorary members of the shop community, staggering in early after their night drives – looking for a toilet, a hot drink and a chat. Each driver must take ridicule for the football team they support, for football is the language spoken here.

'Sprechen sie Fussball?'

They all do – except Michael. Michael doesn't support a team, and refreshingly doesn't pretend to either. His voice is educated and professional. He worked in IT for twenty-five years, before he was made redundant, when the government pulled out of their contracts. He still rages eloquently against the government. Fine words butter no parsnips, however, and so at the age of fifty-one he spent £2,500 of his own money to train for a HGV licence. He is now the unlikeliest of lorry drivers, without a trace of brown sauce on his shirt.

Michael is mucking in because of the way things have fallen. As he says: 'If God gives you lemons, you make lemonade.'

This is so. You may not thank God for the lemons. Indeed, you may say, 'Fuck the lemons, frankly.' But the bills still need paying. So in middle age, Michael left his desk and learned lorry driving. Whether he has learned anything about himself, I don't know.

And Winston, as we know, is also on the move; always about to hand in his notice: 'Do not expect to see me here for much longer, Simon,' says Winston.

I'm not holding my breath, though. There are five seasons every year: summer, autumn, winter, spring — and Winston leaving. In fact, I am surrounded by leavers. Leaving, leaving everywhere — yet everyone still here.

In dull fatherly fashion, I always say the same thing: 'The manager may be a complete shit. But consider your rent. Make sure you have something else in the bag before making the jump; because it's not easy when you don't.'

I speak with feeling when I say this. I had nothing lined up when I left the priesthood, not realising how unemployable a former clergyman is. My writing earned me a little, but was generally rejected by agents, publishers and newspapers alike. I took a cleaning job, and coached one or two Somali children who were falling behind. And I found myself absurdly happy on discovering a fiver on the pavement — a telling moment in my fall from grace. I had traipsed around shop after shop, leaving my CV, but found no interest. They didn't even get back to me to say 'No.' They said they'd be in contact — but never were. I tried one or two fast food outlets as well. But on finding the manager of one to be about twelve, and the staff considerably younger, I knew I was in the wrong place. When someone did actually send a rejection letter, tears came to my eyes in gratitude — gratitude that they had gone to such trouble: 'Thank you for turning me down like this! And headed notepaper as well?! You're so kind.'

(It is of passing interest to note that the only store to offer me a job was the store that did psychometric testing over the phone – and therefore knew nothing about my age or my past.)

. I found it hard when people didn't get back to me; when I was left in limbo. I prefer to know news, good or bad. If I do not know it, my imagination is given too much room for exercise in the fields of unreality, and there is no health there. Imagination is a state between wakefulness and sleep, with the benefits of neither. Once I know the bad news, and have taken the hit, my inner self can practise the art of recovery. 'Hope springs eternal!' is not something to be said to others in their disappointment; it will sound glib, and irritate. But it is a profound personal truth, when our reality is faced and accepted. It may not be what we wish for ourselves, but is what is true for ourselves. We are eternally hopeful and happy people, and here is the beginning of healing. Our inner resources are remarkable, if we feed them the truth.

Why did no one want me? Perhaps they imagined that as an ex-priest, I would preach sermons at them. It is, I admit, an unattractive prospect: obligatory joke, becoming slick anecdote, becoming profound thought, becoming personal challenge, all day, every day, like some interminable radio 'Thought for the day'. Agghh! I could see why no one wanted me. And then of course there is the unspoken feeling that if you have left the priesthood early, it can only be for one reason – and that's a very large elephant to have standing in your room.

I did get one interview at a supermarket, but realised too late that it was for bakery. Instantly, I was racking my brains for 'bread' stories. Had I known the deal in advance, I could have prepared, and invented a childhood of yeasty longing. While others had wanted to be train drivers or footballers, I wished only to follow in my father's footsteps, and be a 'Bread Man'. Yes, I could feel my closing words taking shape:

'I'll never forget the day – the day my father was killed by thieves who broke in to steal a bloomer loaf. As he lay dying in my arms, he said: "Son – you're a baker's boy who just became a man."'

However, I didn't realise it was a bakery interview until too late, and so stayed with the truth. I confessed to no experience of baking. I do remember saying I enjoyed fresh rolls with cheddar as much as the next man, but it didn't hit the spot, and I wasn't offered the job. He said I didn't have enough baking experience, which was a nice way of saying he didn't employ paedophiles. By a happy twist of fate, I often bake in my present store and enjoy it immensely. It took about ten minutes to learn.

The truth is, baking was never a childhood ambition of mine, for I thought only of being George Best. Yet now, baking gives me great satisfaction, while the thought of being George Best palls a little. This suggests to me that too much planning about the future is probably unwise, because we don't know anything; we really don't. I remember the story told by Charles Handy – author, philosopher and keen observer of business organisations. He told of his early experiences in a world-famous multinational company. By way of encouragement to this bright young man, they produced an outline of his future career with them: 'This will be your life,' they said to him, showing him an impressive print-out of future jobs he would hold.

Young Charles contemplated the list, and noticed that the story ended with him as chief executive of a particular company in a far-off country. Well, well, well! He felt flattered at the time – they had such plans for him! He left the company before reaching such dizzy heights, however – noting only that when he did leave, not only did the job picked for him no longer exist, neither did the company he would have directed, nor the country in which he would have operated.

☖ ☖ ☖

Bryn has had to make changes too. He is a young deputy manager, with a huge tie, gelled spiky hair – and presently trying to lead an early morning team briefing in the canteen. He is having trouble with Faith, however. He has just pulled her up for reading *Hello!* magazine while he's talking. Faith is Nigerian, Christian and lippy – and sucks her teeth in disdain.

'And you stop looking at my arse all the time,' she says quietly.

'I beg your pardon?' says Bryn.

'You heard,' says Faith. 'Stop looking at my arse.'

'In your dreams,' he says nervously, while attempting to peel his bulgy eyes away from her curvy backside.

'In your dreams more like,' she says, as she turns another page, smiling.

In Ancient China, pre-1000 BC, the world's first book, the *Book of Changes*, was written specifically with this matter in mind. Primarily a book of divination, it is based on the principle of a synchronised universe that we either work with or against. Should a Prince go to war? Should a trader cross the river with his goods? Should a mother ostracise her son? Should Bryn stop eyeing up Faith?

In the old days, the enquirer visited the Sage who sat with his special twigs. The Sage would receive them, hear of their quandary, place the sticks as he was led by sun, moon and stars, and hey presto! – the constellation of the twigs told all.

Three thousand years later, we live in a supermarket world, where the Sage is just a herb, and a synchronised universe no longer the talk of the town. In the absence of a Sage, Bryn consults his team sheets to discover who's missing – and calls an early morning team briefing.

Before suffering a bad knee injury, he was a semi-pro footballer, with lovely ball skills and a bright future. Leeds United wanted him. But that was then and this is now; instead of the yellow brick road to football stardom, he is wedged inside a small supermarket canteen talking to bored employees about sales figures. And trying to keep his eyes off Faith.

'Got to roll with the punches, Si,' he says to me later, when considering his disappointments. 'Got to roll with the punches.'

For Bryn, there is no synchronicity in his universe – just struggle. His perception of the past is that life has punched him, and punched him hard. So what do you do? You get up, and fight back. You give as good as you get, in the wrestling match that is existence. You try supermarkets – because the money's OK, and the bar is set pretty low for trainee managers. And if that doesn't work out, you fight on – you try something else.

And in time, as we will see, Bryn does try something else.

My biggest change of direction came two years before I left the priesthood. It was huge – though no one knew of it but myself. It happened at 2.00 am one morning, in a bedroom far from home, and happened so quietly that even I might have missed it. I was away on an eight-day silent retreat – the first I had taken for some years. I'd spent much of my time, day after day, in an old art room, drawing pictures of extraordinary rage. I am not a painter – I paint like a child. But you don't need to be skilled in the craft to express your feelings, and this is what I did. It was good to be away from rationalising words, and tapping into something more visceral. Though when I use the word 'good', I describe something awful.

With the bits and pieces life gives us, we build ourselves a house of understanding – and then attempt live in it. It is unlikely to be a very wonderful house – our building material is limited – but it is ours, and familiar, and we will stay in it as long as we possibly can. But every pillar of my particular house had now collapsed, and I was wandering in the ruins, wondering what or who I could trust. Like Bryn, I felt punched hard by life – punched mercilessly, and with no apparent point to the beating, except my inner and outer destruction. 'Strong pillars falling' was my calling card.

This was the priest who went away on silent retreat; this was the human who went away on silent retreat. I had a sense of being cut off from something good. In particular, I could no longer trust – and this is a most crippling condition. In my mind, I had a picture of myself sitting at the edge of a large and unbridgeable chasm. I was on one side of the chasm, and on the other side was trust. Between us was a deep hole quite impossible for me to cross. All I seemed to have in my pocket was the ruins of a past life – and desperate rage. Hope? You must be joking! And so it was I went to sleep.

There is nothing to report, in a way. Just that I woke up at 2.00 am, after a brief dream in which everything changed. And the difference was this – I woke up on the other side of the chasm. I was rather unformed; a foetus lying there, and barely moving. But I was there; somehow or other the chasm was crossed. Nothing in my life had changed on the face of it. I would return to an external life unaltered in the smallest detail. But everything had changed. From here, I would trust this life, and all it revealed. Perhaps I had not been punched. Perhaps instead I had been released like a butterfly from sweaty hands? Perhaps this severe mercy was something about synchronicity? Time would tell: 'Test your mountain experience on Monday,' as they say.

Interestingly, on the last day of retreat, my childish painting turned from cages and imprisonment to a marketplace overladen with fruit. I spent the morning drawing and colouring every wonderful fruit under the sun. How apt then, that on my first day in the supermarket, I should be taken by the manager to the produce section and told: 'This is your empire.'

I looked at the shelves of fruit before me – it was just like my painting. I had come home.

$$\boxminus \quad \boxminus \quad \boxminus$$

Sometimes I stumble from the path of trust. On one or two days since, I have gone into meltdown – when a piece of bad news has affected me with inappropriate force. But this is what I find: if I stay with the terror I experience, it is soon revealed to be an impermanent thing. It is not a monster, but a ghost. Dr Moshe Feldenkrais was a physicist and judo master who taught himself to walk again after a disabling knee injury. At fifty, he gave up his physics career, and dedicated the last thirty years of his life to the art of human movement. He said this: 'The only thing permanent about our behaviour is the belief that it is so.'

And so my thoughts return to Michael, our lorry driver. The team briefing is over, and as we unload his truck early in the day, all things are ahead of us. How will the day go? If you had said to Michael five years ago that he'd be a supermarket man, he'd have laughed in your face – or cried. He knew where his life was going; he was an IT specialist, and that was that. But maybe we are unwise to place permanence in our heads as an ideal. And Michael seems content enough now, amid the usual chaos of the early hours in the shop. I watch him sip his coffee, and as the caffeine enters his veins, a smile breaks across his face. He is perking up, which is just as well, for the day holds other journeys for him, with many miles to go before he sleeps.

And he is not alone in that. Together we shall seize this supermarket day!

2.

A Fragile Beginning

In which Simon sets out, and Garry
finds the keys. We hear the strange
tale of the Christmas tree; Bryn looks
for distraction, Ola proposes to Sapphy
— and you know what? It's all a bit
like the beginning of time.

I will begin again.

This is my thought as I climb the dark hill, on my way to work. It is early, and young Polish men with rucksacks wait on corners to be collected by vans which pull up, open up and then pull away. I prefer to walk, though sometimes Big Sam draws up alongside me, in the car he can't afford, and gives me a lift. He doesn't come today, because of health problems — in fact, he's been away from the shop for weeks. And, anyway, I notice more when I walk. This morning, the wallflower spills purple through masonry cracks with great optimism, and I sense something similar in myself. I'm off to work — and work for me is a supermarket, where I will stack shelves, work on the till and change the world.

Supermarkets! They have come a long way from their humble origins. Once they were a wheelbarrow of fruit in a north of England market; or a small stall in London's East End; or a corner shop selling dairy products. These days, they rule the world, and governments grovel before them. (Tesco is even big in Shanghai, where they sell live toads – something they don't do at their branch in East Cheam.) Yet however huge you are, and however massive – if you are a shop, you still have to open on time. You may have the ear of Prime Ministers, and the profits of Croesus, but someone still has to rummage through their pockets for the keys, turn them in the lock and get the show on the road. And this morning, that man is Garry.

Garry is waiting for me at the shop. Garry is my friend, similar in age, and a companion in hair loss. He waits for me, because there must be two present when the store is opened, just in case trouble awaits inside. Garry is not so bright this morning, because he drank too much last night.

'I made a whorehouse of my liver,' he says, with slight regret.

But here's a thing – however much Garry drinks, he's always at work the next day. Some people look for any excuse not to come in, but he looks only to be here. Somewhere in his psyche, he likes to work, needs to work, and when he's not working, or downloading films, he drifts towards the pub – or goes on holiday to Greece, where he dances on tables long into the night. He says that he might live there one day.

'I tell you, Si,' he says, 'that's the life. That is the fucking life.'

It may be the life – but it feels some distance away, as in the morning chill Garry fumbles in his pocket for the keys. He's taking a while, and not just because of the hangover. Due to a number of recent burglaries, there are more keys and locks than there used to be. In fact, it may not be the time to mention it, because it is a sore subject – but our store has experienced something of a crime fest in recent weeks.

'We should just give money away at the door,' says Garry.

Managers from other stores talk of us in hushed tones and with ill-concealed mirth: '£2,000 taken from the cash office after Sunday trading one week. And then, wait for it – £15,000 taken two weeks later, after a night break-in! Is the store run by monkeys or something?'

Many of us think monkeys would do a better job than our managers. But I have to say, we were all very surprised at who the culprit turned out to be; very surprised indeed.

'You just don't know people,' everyone said to everyone else, the morning we found out. 'You just do not know people.'

Why did they do it? None of us could understand. But there will be more of that in a later chapter, when we've met all the suspects.

The worst theft I experienced as a priest was when someone cut the Church Christmas tree in half. Each year, and with some difficulty, we put up a huge Christmas tree outside the front of the church and covered it with lights. It looked sparkly and magical as people made their way home on the dark December nights.

I'd turn the lights off last thing. The Vicarage was next to the church, so it was a short walk and a pleasing evening ritual. I'd then rise early in the morning to turn them on again. Until one day it became apparent through the deep dawn dark that the tree had been sawn in half during the night. Who had done such a thing? Simple police work carried out by me and my Dalmatian, Sydney, revealed that the top half of the tree had been dragged along the pavement to a squat up the road – the type that have pyjama tops for curtains and throb with music at 4.00 am. The following night, the squatters came back for the lights – breaking a door to get to the socket. They wanted Christmas on the cheap, which is a shame in a way, because the real Christmas is free.

I didn't call the police, however.

'Have you called the police?' everyone said.

I didn't call the police because sometimes sadness is beyond the reparation of the law. They may have flashing lights on their cars, and back-up round the corner in case of trouble, but they couldn't mend our Christmas tree; and only we could mend our hearts. So we journeyed on through Advent with our stump – our Christmas stump. In time, like the bleak stable of the Christmas story, 'Stumpy' acquired his own charm – the children wrote stories about him, and a woman asked if we could have a stump every year.

'It speaks to me,' she said, seeing my quizzical look. 'We're all missing something.'

But that is in the past. This morning, my present is with Garry, and the beginnings of a supermarket day. Across the country, people are opening their eyes, hitting alarm clocks, groaning, turning over, going back to sleep, showering with a song, jogging to music, banging on the bathroom door in some desperation, doing t'ai chi in public parks, wondering if life will get better, making plans – perhaps some are smiling. Does how we begin our day have any effect on the outcome?

'Start each day like a newcomer to the world,' someone once said to me. 'Like an innocent in a wonderful land.'

For myself, I would like to wake with more delight than I do, and yes, with more wonder. My dreams are rarely peaceful, and often restless. So I have a morning ritual. Once up, I make a cup of strong coffee, and then enjoy a meditation, followed by a morning run through empty streets. Much better! Now all things seem possible, and the supermarket day unbearably hopeful. The genius lies in holding on to the hope when the day begins to shit on you – as soon it does.

Finally, Garry cracks the locks, and we enter the building. Ahh! It's like entering a temple, silent and full of shadows. Like a theatre before the players and audience arrive, the shop space is hushed, still and waiting. It's a moment to be treasured, for this peaceful calm will soon be a hubbub of worried lives in brief and hurried conjunction.

Oh, the emotional energy that will pass through this place before the day is done! Enough power to heat a small town through winter. For now, however, there is only the low hum of the freezers. No one's here; the store is in darkness, and it's like the beginning of time. Like a cathedral at midnight, the aisles are un-peopled and the tills full only of air. The CCTV cameras discreetly film nothing, recording absence for posterity. 'Before some thing, no thing,' as they said in Ancient China. But will the day go well?

'I've got some shit on my shoe,' says Garry, discerning the source of an unpleasant smell. 'I hate dog shit.'

I tell him to stand still while I go off to find some tissue, and as I scurry towards the toilets, I find myself remembering my daughter. On her very first walk outside – her first brave and faltering steps in the world, taken in the heart of London – she too trod in shit. As I wiped it off her bright red sandals, and got some on my hands, I had the urge to say: 'This is how it is. Get used to it.'

But why pass my despair on to her, disguising it as wisdom? She would face her own despair, in her own way, and find her own answers. With the shit cleared, her bright red shoes were lovely once again.

🛒 🛒 🛒

Ten minutes later, and Bryn – all gel, spiky hair and white socks – is in the office. He's on the early shift and trying to print out yesterday's takings. This is important, because a supermarket judges its existence by its takings. Good takings, good day; bad takings, bad day – it's a simple if dull equation. Bryn is easily distracted, however, and watches the female staff as they walk past the door. He's hoping someone will come in and interrupt him. He doesn't like it when it's quiet; too much time to think makes him unsettled. Perhaps he'll go and swagger round Faith or Sapphy, who are both easy on the eye. Or perhaps he'll have a boys' conversation with the lads. He wants someone to put their head round the door and say: 'Oh Bryn – I'm glad it's you on Earlies! We love it when you're on Earlies!'

But no one does, because no one's looking out for anyone else at present. We are all too fragile – too unsure as to who or why we are. We are shop workers, but beyond that? Most were very recently in bed, and got to the bus without conscious thought. We are here, but we are not here; awake but asleep. We can remember who we were yesterday, but what of today? Identity can be elusive in the first moments of the day; and the strong impressions of yesterday, lost. It's almost as if we don't exist. Amid such uncertainty, the vending machine becomes the holy shrine, bestowing hot sweet blessing. Cups of tea and hot chocolate are cradled in shaky hands, as we meander down calm and empty aisles.

Only one person is truly awake – Ola.

'Ah – my bride!' declares Ola.

Ola is the cleaner, who is already well into his day. He moves round the shop floor with his massive cleaning machine, like it's a Ferrari. He pulls up alongside Sapphy, who is loitering by the magazines.

'Ah – my bride! You will be my bride!'

'Fuck off, Ola.' Sapphy really doesn't need this so early in the day. She hardly even knows him, though he does have a nice body, and it is good to be wanted, and she's feeling better about herself already, but all men are pigs, though some are nice, and she's Greek-Cypriot, and he's Nigerian, so that's not going to work, though he is quite sweet, but there's no way they could be an item, absolutely no way, though never say never.

'We will get married!' he says.

They haven't been out – let alone stayed in. They haven't done anything! But Ola promises to buy her nice clothes for their wedding in Nigeria. *Nigeria?* She likes the idea of the nice clothes, sure – but perhaps not those particular nice clothes.

'I doan even know yah!' she says, in pure Cockney.

'You will get to know me.'

'Oh yeah? An wha' if I doan like yah?! Then wha'?'

'You do not understand – but you will, you will.'

'Whatevaa!' she says, and turns back towards the magazines.

'The only aisle you'll walk her down is the meat aisle,' says Faith, both Ola's friend and critic.

'Shut your mouth, woman!'

'You shut your mouth, you rude man! Harassing the poor girl! It's too early to propose!'

'Not when you've been up since five am.'

Ola does not wish to be driving this cleaning machine; in his head he's a businessman. He wants to be a businessman in England – better still, a businessman in Nigeria, where his mum ran an import business. But the company was crippled by corruption – backhanders to all and sundry – and he can't face the same struggle. So he cleans night and day in a faraway land, to pay for his business course. And one day he'll be a businessman here and he'll marry Sapphy – when finally she understands.

Or perhaps he'll marry someone else. Who knows? After all, it's early and, like the start of time – when the cosmos lay unformed, and all was potential and possibility – nothing is certain at the day's fragile beginning.

3.

It's All the Rage, Apparently!

In which Banana Woman sounds off;
Winston winds up the customers;
customers wind up Simon — and
sanctuary is found by the eggs.

We've only just opened, and there's a woman going bananas by the bananas.

'This place is like the bloody third world!' she is shouting. 'I mean look at the shelves – look at them!'

The shelves are a little empty, I agree, but there's not a lot we can do. There was a fire at our main delivery depot two days ago, since when we haven't had a proper delivery. We're getting other stores' leftovers, basically – and Banana Woman isn't happy.

'Call this a shop?!' she shouts at me, and as she's the first customer of the day, her voice echoes across the store, waking several members of staff.

'I'm afraid there was a fire at our depot on Sunday,' I explain, 'and we're still recovering. We're hoping for a better delivery today.'

'It's like the bloody third world,' she says, returning to her theme. 'The bloody third world!'

And with that farewell, she is gone – a hurricane of upset leaving behind due desolation. She has offended the two-thirds of the staff who are from the third world; and made uncomfortable the other third, who know that many there would love shelves as full as our 'empty' ones.

But what does Banana Woman care? She's thrown her tantrum and moved on. Welcome to angry land.

Anger – it's all the rage apparently, and evident not only in customers. As we know, Winston once had the ambition to be rich and married by the age of thirty-three. Ideally, he would also have opened the bowling for the West Indies. These were his hopes. He is now forty, single, poor and one thing I didn't mention – walks with a permanent limp. So there's plenty of room for resentment. And as if that isn't enough, he is also quietly furious to be on the till again this morning.

He looks out with frustration at the shop floor. Other staff members are allowed endless freedom to roam, while he is trapped behind this high-tech money box. He feels unappreciated in this store; just as he has never been appreciated. Consider his predicament: only recently, he was taken away from cosy office duties, for absolutely no reason – no reason at all! And yet neither, it seems, is he welcome on the shop floor. Well, really!

How will calm but angry Winston respond? It's almost too obvious: he'll take it out on the customer. He'll say everything he is meant to say, because the management have recently been giving him grief. But there are ways of doing things correctly that drive the customers mad. And – oh dear

– here comes a customer now:

Winston begins to pass their goods through, until he gets to the fruit juice.

'If sir were to buy another carton of fruit juice, he'd be eligible for our free gift.'

This is correct behaviour. We are told to promote sales on the tills, by tempting customers with free gifts.

'But I don't want another carton of fruit juice,' says the customer, eager to be on his way.

'No,' says Winston. 'But if sir did buy another one, he'd get a free gift. It's worth considering.'

'What's the free gift?'

'A children's sandwich box.'

'What would I want with a children's sandwich box?'

'They're very popular.'

'I don't have any children.'

'There's a choice of four colours.'

'But I don't want one.'

'I think we may be out of the yellow ones.'

'I don't want a children's sandwich box!'

'And it's free with an extra carton of fruit juice.'

'Look. Why would I buy an extra carton of fruit juice I don't want, to get a free gift I don't want?'

'It's completely up to sir.'

Of course, Winston was removed from the office because he was a nightmare to work with and made constant accounting errors. And he's not stacking shelves now because he can't do that either. He gets impatient, and if he can't immediately see the correct place for an item, he'll put it somewhere else – because in the end, what's the big deal about where something goes, as long as it's on a shelf somewhere? Let the customers look for it if they really want it!

What's round and aggressive? A vicious circle – and it's such a circle that Winston painfully walks. His low self-esteem crucifies him daily. He determinedly doesn't care, for that would be to give value to things – and he can't allow that. If he doesn't have value himself, then nothing else will either. Equally, however, he is hurt daily by people criticising or rejecting him – for what he wants most of all is to be valued; and beyond that, loved.

'Want any help, Simon?' he asks, looking for work on the shop floor.

The answer is that I don't. Or rather, I do, but not from him. Eternity's too short for help from Winston. 'I think we're OK thanks, Winston.'

I feel uncomfortable, but am aware how long it takes to undo his uncaring work. And he's not someone who can ever be told anything; not by staff or customers. Listen to another encounter on the till: 'Thank you for waiting, madam,' he says, as the customer approaches him.

Again, this is something we are supposed to say to any customer who's been standing in a queue. But this lady hasn't been – she has come straight from the shop floor.

'I haven't waited,' she says.

'Thank you anyway,' he says, giving no ground.

'What are you thanking me for?'

'I'm thanking you for waiting, madam.'

'But I haven't waited!'

Winston just smiles knowingly, which irritates her all the more.

'I haven't waited! There was no queue,' she says, sounding increasingly like Basil Fawlty.

'Whatever you say, madam, whatever you say. But thank you anyway.'

Winston's self-image is of a calm and reasonable man. This means that his trapped anger must seep out through the hidden channels of passive-aggression. As someone said, 'Denial is not a river in Egypt, but a fucking ocean – and we're all drowning.'

Certainly Winston's journey through life would be a good deal happier if he faced this crippling force in his life – but there are many Winstons out there.

A refusal to acknowledge the issue of anger is often the sign of children who perceive themselves to have been ignored or rejected by their parents. Unable to take their parents on – which really would be the last battle – they close down on themselves, in easy-going self-rejection. They cannot value themselves, so they sure as eggs won't value anything else.

'Nothing matters!'

Winston's mood is lightened if the West Indies triumph at cricket. But even this grand passion is distorted by negativity, and shaped more by hate than love. He is happier still if England lose; he is happier if England lose than if the West Indies win.

🛒 🛒 🛒

I have mentioned the rage which caught me unawares on retreat some years back. It was like finding a seething cauldron in my front room. Somehow – who knows how? – I had managed to ignore it to this point. But then we ignore all things, until ready to face them. If you had asked me before this time, I would, like Winston, have denied anger:

'Are you going to take the lid off the cauldron, Simon – and look inside?'

'Cauldron? What cauldron? I don't know what you're talking about.'

'Are you going to take the lid off the cauldron, Simon – and look inside?'

'I don't see any cauldron! Something small in the corner, maybe, but it's nothing.'

'Are you going to take the lid off the cauldron, Simon – and look inside?'

'There may be something cauldron-shaped here – it's hard to tell in this light.'

'Are you going to take the lid off the cauldron, Simon – and look inside?'

'Oh, *that* cauldron!'

It's a conversation that can take years and years and years.

I may be putting out the parsnips now, all white and rooty, but I still remember the Bishop who told me that if he let his anger out, it would pull down the whole world. It's a striking image from a spiritual leader, and a reminder that status in society is quite irrelevant in the matter of unexamined rage. It is also a reminder of why some so fear their rage – they are concerned for what they might unleash or do. As children, they feared to rock the boat, and take this fear into their adult lives. Keep the lid on the cauldron at all costs!

But more frightening by far than facing the rage, is not facing it. For exiled anger, unacknowledged and repressed, seeps like poison into every relationship – a thought which passes through my mind later in the day, when a large man approaches me on the till. He's heaving two trolley loads of shopping, and this could be a problem. It's policy in this store always to ask customers if they wish to have a bag – it's a 'green' thing. On this occasion, however, I fear the outcome:

'Would you like a bag, sir?' I ask, as I begin to work through his trolley load.

'What?'

I sense the anger rising. 'Would you like a bag?'

'Course I want a fucking bag! How else will I fucking get it home?'

It's a fair point, in its way.

'We just have to ask, sir,' I say. 'We're trying to cut down on the bags we use. New green policy.'

'Green policy? Everywhere I go, it's do do this, and don't do that! Fucking waste of time. I'll have as many bags as it takes.'

'It's something about the planet, I suppose.'

'What was that?!'

'The planet. It's about looking after the ice cap, and Bangladesh and, er, the penguins...'

'Never mind the fucking penguins, mate. You just look after my shopping. I was over-charged last week. Was that green policy too?'

I feel trapped behind the till, in the face of this untreated rage – and Faith kindly comforts me, sneering at the man as he leaves.

'Rude, rude man,' she says.

🛒 🛒 🛒

I like good anger. Good anger's great.

Like polished silver, anger can be beautiful; dissociated from the ego, rage can be a most wonderful thing. As Gandhi showed, when anger has no owner or director, it is clarity and power; a cleansing, exposing and redeeming presence. Such anger is conscious anger; not lashing out in personal affront, but precise in its dealings. Here is anger accurately aimed at appropriate targets – like the figure of Jesus sweeping through the Temple precincts in Jerusalem, overturning the tables of the money lenders and exploitative vendors. Wonderful stuff – and nothing at all like Banana Woman.

I withdraw to the eggs. This is where I go when my ego rages with personal affront. The eggs are to be found in a far corner of the shop, and off the beaten track. Customers can never find them, which can cause irritation – but for me, they are sanctuary. Sometimes I am on my knees there, reaching through to the back where the broken eggs lie smashed and smelly; I enjoy cleaning them up, with cloth and cleaning fluid. Sometimes I have to get up off my knees and go and find the scraper to attack the dried egg on the floor. But generally, I simply stack the eggs. There is a meditative and ordering quality to stacking egg boxes, one on top of the other, row after row – large, medium, organic. So this is where I go to allow mad emotions to pass through me; to allow a sense of personal grievance to disperse. I am in touch again with my breathing, and present things. How can I not be happy?

Sometimes, when it's all the rage, it's good to go eggs-directory.

4.

LOVE, LUST AND SWOONING

In which Sapphy declares Bryn a pervert and Caspar displays skulduggery on the tills. Winston swoons, and Faith makes an indecent proposal. But not to Simon — who was probably more attractive as a priest.

Bryn, the deputy manager of the gelled and spiky hair, likes checking figures – of the female variety. The female staff know all about him 'running his eyes over their section'.

'It's right pervy!' declares Sapphy.

'He's a bloke,' says Caspar. 'It's natural.'

'Men!'

'What – and you never look at anyone?'

'Not like that, I doan!'

'Oh yeah – you just want bubble bath and roses, I suppose?'

'It'd be a good start.'

'Men are different – they cut to the chase when they look at girls.'

'It's like he's mentally undressing me!'

'So?'

Sapphy is probably complaining to the wrong person – for

Caspar is a full-time woman-watcher. He tells me he knows all women within a one-mile radius of the store. When I say he knows them, he knows two things about them. He knows if he fancies them, and whether he has a chance. He heads a small posse of male employees with similar interests – of which Bryn is a member. The posse employ me as an outrider. As I work next to the window which looks out onto the street, it is my role to spot any 'talent' by the bus stop – and let them know. I once saw Caspar and Bryn almost crush an old lady as they steamed out of the warehouse on 'skirt alert'. Caspar knows I'm not always reliable; that often I am too engrossed in my broccoli or mushrooms to pay full attention to the bus stop beauties. But this seems not to matter, as even when I do run and find him, he usually knows already.

'Where women are concerned, Si, I have radar.'

Caspar is twenty-one, and likes young women – but doesn't close the door on those who are older. The word to describe such women is MILF – mothers I'd like to… And though he says that thirty-five is his upper limit, there's no way his roving eye keeps to that.

Caspar is undoubtedly a sharp operator, and can even pull a bird on the till. Yes, he's been known to get a girl's number even as he serves her, which is a matter for great respect from all male employees under the age of twenty-five. But there's also skulduggery behind the charm as the following incident reveals:

Here's the first fact: when serving on the tills, your eyes do tend to wander down the queue, to see who's coming your way. The second fact follows on from the first: some in the queue are more attractive than others, and you obviously wish to get these at your till. With our 'one queue' system, however – like in post offices and banks – you don't know who you're going to get until the last minute. Sometimes, you may have to stall a little with one customer to get the one you're after. This is not hard. You just take an age to find the flower bag, or to sort out their change, until the unwanted customer is safely off to another till. Then you are ready to swoop. Your finger moves quickly to the button. 'Please go to Till Number One,' says the recorded voice. Result!

And here's another fact: there is a massage parlour up the road, with agendas way beyond a quick rub. Sometimes the girls from there come to us for refreshment, because everyone needs a break. They are usually foreign, very attractive – and all means, fair and foul, will be used by the male employees to land them on their till.

The other day, an old lady was ahead of one of these girls. The young woman's skirt was unbearably short, and all male eyes were on her. Oblivious to this, the old lady goes to Caspar's till. Exhausted by so much walking, carrying and standing, she dumps her heavy load down with some relief.

'Hello, young man,' she says to Caspar. And then adds jokily: 'Got time for an old'un?'

But Caspar doesn't have time for an old'un; right now, he's got no time for her at all. 'You must go to him,' he says, pointing the old lady in my direction.

'What?' she asks, suddenly confused.

'You must go to him,' he repeats, dead-eyed but urgent. He knows it's a race against time. 'I am unable to serve you at the present time, due to circumstances.'

Circumstances? What circumstances?! With a resigned shrug, the old lady wheezes, picks up her basket, lugs it over to my till, and dumps it down on my serving shelf. I am not pleased. I am moments away from the massage-parlour queen, and my first thought is to send her back to Caspar. I relent, however, as the beads of sweat break out on her forehead. She might not make it back.

Caspar wins again.

But it's not just Caspar who falls in lust on the tills. Winston has his own story to tell. He is not a natural sexual predator, peering uncertainly through his glasses, in his ill-fitting uniform. But put a voluptuous lady in front of him and his firework is lit, and fizzing into the sky. As he tells me: 'Pretty ladies I can serve, Simon, no problem. But voluptuous? Then I buckle.'

He recounts how, recently, he was stunned by the eyes of a woman he was serving.

'I am telling you, Simon – I could not take my eyes away from hers. It was like they were glued.'

'So how did you serve her?'

'I don't know. I really don't know. But I completed the transaction, and then tried to settle myself. I felt my throat tightening, but went into my usual routine. "Your receipt, madam; your change, madam; your eyes, ma–" I stopped there. I was so embarrassed at what had slipped out.'

'You said, "Your eyes, madam"?'

'I did, yes. I don't know where it came from.'

'Well, I'm not sure that's such a mystery.'

'It is to me.'

'So what did she do?' I asked.

'The woman? She didn't do anything. She just smiled.'

'Perhaps checkout assistants always say that sort of thing to her.'

'Well I don't always say that sort of thing! Not at all!'

'No.'

Winston was shocked by himself; shocked at his breakdown in the face of beauty; disturbed by the power of those eyes to create in him in such yearning for something unknown – the little child searching still.

But it's not always easy to spot the difference between lust and friendship. And it all started with prayer.

Faith had called me over to the biscuits.

'I need your prayers,' she said to me.

I had survived for a year in the store with no one knowing I'd been a priest. I was grateful for this. I wished to come with a clean slate, and be known only for who I was, rather than for roles I'd played. One might think it would be a hard thing to hide – the missing twenty years on my CV – but strangely, no one asked. I ask questions all the time, but no one asked them of me. So for a year at least, I was just another super-market worker, which was great. But then someone hears from someone who'd heard from someone else, and those who are interested respond. Like Faith, for instance.

'I need your prayers.'

'Really?' I say, a little hesitantly.

'I've been listening to this Christian radio station. It's very good; very helpful – because life is difficult.'

'It is, yes.'

'They read the Bible to you, and encourage you to pray more when life is hard.'

I made some non-committal but affirming noises about how I was glad that she found it helpful, and that yes, our worries could pile up, and that no decisions were ever straightforward, and that it was reassuring to find a place of peace sometimes, and to trust the way ahead, and that yes, everyone was lonely sometimes.

'But God is good!' she said.

'God is good,' I agreed.

'He will provide!'

I smiled, and didn't see her again until the next day, when I was talking to Caspar by the mangoes. He was telling me that he was in-between girlfriends. Faith then approached us, and joined in the conversation.

'I don't know whether I'm with her or not,' said Caspar.

'You not with your girlfriend?' she asks.

'It's a bit uncertain at present.'

Would Faith offer to pray with him?

'Then I will fuck you,' she says. 'Until things are sorted out.'

God moves in mysterious ways, and here He is, providing for both their needs.

Caspar is pleased with the offer, because though thirty-five, Faith is an attractive woman, and you should never say never. But there are caveats. First, she did have three children, and Caspar had played computer games with her eldest boy of seventeen. So that felt a bit odd, because what would he say? And then Faith's brother is a trainee manager in the store, who could be a bit of a shit, and what would happen if he knew that Caspar had done his sister? You had to consider these things. And finally, though it is a tempting offer – is she really serious?

In the circumstances, I feel a bit of a gooseberry – all too aware that Faith had only asked for prayer from me. There are degrees of intimacy on offer – prayer on one side, sex on the other, and a chasm in between.

'I must get on,' I say.

'Where you going, man?' asks Caspar.

I am uncomfortable, and eager to be away, but Caspar wants me to stay. He doesn't know what to say to Faith, and I am a convenient distraction.

'Si's had a run-in with the manager,' he says, by way of nothing at all; and it was hardly what Faith wanted to hear, given the offer she'd just made.

For myself, I was probably more attractive as a priest. I remember the first person I told, after making my decision to get ordained.

'I am going to become a priest,' I said.

I did not know her well, and we were standing in a busy high street. But I suppose I expected quiet words of congratulation or spiritual affirmation. Instead, she said: 'Then you will need to be very aware of the women. They will come for you.'

I nodded sagely as she spoke – as though this was a problem I had wrestled with long into the night – while really thinking: 'Chance would be a fine thing.'

She turned out to be right, however. Presumably it's the uniform, the mystery, the unobtainability and the fact that, sometimes, you actually appear to be listening. Whatever, the priest quickly enters into the parishioners' sexual fantasies. I remember an Iranian woman in a tower block, who said she had fantasies about me and the Pope. This would have been more affirming, had the Pope at the time not been in his eighties.

There was another woman who also told me of her dreams: 'So there I was, in bed with you.'

'Really?'

'And we were absolutely naked.'

'Well, there's a thing.'

'Stark naked!'

'It really must have been a dream!'

'You had chosen me to join you!'

'Had I?'

'Quite surprised, I was! You chose me!'

'Dreams. Mad, aren't they? Absolutely crazy! Now about the

prayers on Sunday, Jacquie...'

But those days are gone. Today, standing behind a till, Caspar can pull anything, and I can't even pull a curtain. Boom, boom!

5.

GROCERY MISCONDUCT

In which Sapphy has £100 stolen by a
colleague and Simon has an awkward
meeting with Pinocchio, the truth-shy
manager. Rosemary makes a child cry
— and we hear of the man who slides
miles on his knees in search of heaven.

Sapphy is finding things hard this morning. She is bored, of course,
but then she's always bored. She aches for life to hurry on so she
can be somewhere other than where she is now.

'I'm so bored, Si! 'Ow am I goin' ter make it ter free
o'clock? I juzz doan know 'ow I'm goin' ter get froo today!'

But today, she's not only bored — she's also fuming. She had
£100 stolen yesterday by a work colleague; and now he's next
to her on the tills. Here's what happened: when leaving
yesterday, she nipped into the toilet, and left £100 holiday
money there in an envelope.

'I doan know why I did that — I really doan!'

She then left the store and got on a bus, before she realised
what she'd done.

'I fort "Oh my God!" and told the bus driver to stop immediately!'

She was back in the store within ten minutes, and rushed to the toilet – but the money was gone.

'This was me 'oliday money! Me 'oliday money for Cyprus.'

CCTV footage revealed that four people had used the toilet since she left. Their lockers were duly searched, but the thief had thought of that. What was strange was that none of the 'film footage four' was searched on leaving. This seemed something of an oversight, but the manager appeared to be losing no sleep. He thought Sapphy was a bit of a whinger anyway.

'Get over it!' was his attitude, though had it been his money, there would have been strip searches for all staff – and probably customers as well. He was tighter than a yachtsman's knot.

Within twelve hours, the staff had reconstructed events, knew exactly who the thief was, and where the money had been hidden. It was too late for Sapphy, of course. With the money now off the premises, there was no proof of anything, and the manager wished to 'move on' – the compulsive reaction of one who simply didn't want to face the truth, and the truth was this: he had done nothing, because basically, he didn't care.

Sapphy's mum had exploded over the phone yesterday, and said she was coming in. The manager reassured her that the police were involved, which calmed her in the moment – but turned out not to be true. The police were never involved.

The manager wished to move on, not only because he didn't care and had lied with weasel words; but also because the thief was a handy worker in the warehouse.

So this is why Sapphy is scowling on the tills this morning – stood next door to the man who now has £100 of her holiday money at home. He's trying to make small talk with her; trying to have a laugh and a joke. Sapphy doesn't reply; she's really very good at blanking people.

'Why aren't you talking to me?' the thief asks in mock-desperation. 'Women!'

Garry and I are talking later. There have been a few staff-on-staff thefts of late, but none on our shift. Until yesterday.

'It's hard when you can't trust your colleagues,' he says.

Sapphy joins us.

'How are you feeling?' I ask.

'He's standing there, trying to be all chatty! I carn stan' it!'

'That's very hard.'

'We ought to do something,' says Garry.

'What can we do?' I ask. 'There's no proof of anything, and the money's long gone.'

'I s'pose I should be more trusting,' says Sapphy.

'Why?'

'Well, it's good to trust, innit?'

'No,' I say.

'You a former priest saying it's not good to trust!'

'Trust isn't something we do, Sapphy. It's something others give us.'

It's not the first time I've heard this nonsense; heard someone talking of trust as though it is something to aspire to; something towards which we should strain every moral fibre. Trust is not an achievement – it's a gift. It is something bestowed on us by others. When someone so graces our lives that we find ourselves trusting them – it is not something we have done; but something they have done. Their goodness has drawn trust from us, like a trawler draws the gulls. And this was how it had seemed on our shift – until yesterday.

🛒 🛒 🛒

In the meantime, in my capacity as chair of the shop union, I have a difficult meeting in prospect with Pinocchio, our manager. I will talk elsewhere of my appointment to this exalted role – and, for the moment, speak of Pinocchio. He is a young man who is not greatly concerned with what happens in the world – as long as he rises in the company. He was not called Pinocchio by his parents, of course, but acquired the name here, as it slowly dawned on us that everything he says is a lie. He says what he needs to say, to get out of a scrape – but once away, it's basically: 'So long, sucker!'

He is a restless soul, and always on the move. He loves to declare virtuous schemes at the morning briefing; or tell us he'll get right back to us about our latest good idea. But the virtuous schemes never happen, and he never gets back to us. Initially, we called him 'The Boy' – a man, yes, but somehow emotionally still in short trousers. Gradually, however, as his problem with the truth became apparent, 'Pinocchio' stuck.

Pinocchio hates his weekly meetings with me, and always tries to avoid them. He feels I complain all the time; I feel he avoids things all the time. He thinks I'm just interested in how people are treated; I think he's just interested in profit – truly, we are a marriage made in hell. And if it's possible, things are about to worsen. For as I sit with him now, I am wondering whether I should mention the lies; whether I should finally tell him, clearly and without hesitation, that they make it hard for people to trust him – or indeed even listen to him.

'It's like someone pissing in my ear, when he talks,' says Garry, and he's right – that's just what it's like.

'We're here for one reason, Simon,' says Pinocchio, kicking things off. 'To make money. It's as simple as that. That's the only reason we're here, why you and I are sat in this room – and I don't see the point of talking about anything else.'

'You won't make any money with no staff,' I say, aware that the turnover of staff is very high in our store.

'Look. I just want people to do a good day's work. Is that bad? Why do we have all this moaning?'

He is referring to widespread discontent about the attitude of certain managers. 'The union should be coming up with new commercial ideas,' he continues. 'That's the whole point of it, isn't it?'

This is true in a way. It is why the company created their own in-house union. But it's not my vision.

'The trouble is,' I say, 'you won't achieve anything if you treat your staff poorly. Manik, the duty manager, is a nightmare. We had nine individual complaints about him last month.'

'Leave that with me,' says Pinocchio.

'You say "Leave that with me", but the fact is that when we do leave things with you, nothing actually happens.'

'Then you'll just have to trust me.'

'Trust you?'

'Yes – clearly there are issues of confidentiality here – I can't divulge to you my dealings with Manik.'

'Of course.'

'So you should be telling the rest of the staff everything is OK. That's your job.'

'No, that isn't my job, because we have a problem – no one actually believes you any longer, Paul. They don't believe anything you say.'

'I don't know what you mean.'

'I mean that you lie too often for anyone to trust you.'

'Lie?' he says, genuinely shocked.

I hadn't been planning on going this far. Indeed, I'm suddenly wondering if I will have a job at lunchtime; the company supports management in any dispute, and 'liar' is generally an unacceptable accusation.

'It is the widely held perception,' I continue. 'And it doesn't make my job any easier. I need to be able to believe you, in order to tell others that everything is OK.'

He is a little put out, and returns quickly to the confidentiality issue, and how hard it is for a man in his position, blah, blah, blah, and the need to juggle and balance so many issues, etc etc, and how much is done behind the scenes which can't always been seen, blah, blah, after which we build a few fake bridges, before winding the meeting up. It hadn't been one of our better ones.

I return to the shop floor, both to check on the produce section, and to wonder, 'What now?' Did he mind being called a liar? Was he on the phone to HR discussing the procedure for instant dismissal? Apparently not. Time revealed that he didn't seem to mind at all. From his perspective, he'd got through another meeting and the profits were good this week, and he'd avoided the Manik issue – so let's 'move on'.

🛒 🛒 🛒

Just then, Rosemary – our tiny, glam but rather poisonous Jehovah's Witness from Ghana – walks quickly past me. She was on a till, but has now left it, and her reason is soon apparent. She has seen a child.

Rosemary really loves children – this is a fact. It is well known in the store that when she isn't sneaking an extra fifteen minutes for her lunch break, she's loving children.

'I love you,' she says, to every child of four or under who comes into the store. She will drop everything to say 'Hello' to them. If she is talking with me, she will cut me dead in order to get to the toddler.

'Hello, my little one! How are you today?'

It's called 'Cutey duty' by some.

The other thing to say about Rosemary is that she makes children cry. She loves children, but she also makes them cry. It doesn't start out like this — but often ends that way. I watch her now as she smothers the child and parent in adulation. The mothers tend to enjoy this more than the offspring, because life is hard and it's nice to be fussed over a little. But for Rosemary, it's really about the children. Every child is her special love.

'You're my special boy, aren't you?' she coos.

She does make them cry, though, because she plays tricks on them. First, she gains the trust of the child, by engaging them with kind words, and a little adventure. Perhaps she will lead them over to the banana stand or something. Once there, however, her tone changes. She says something in mock-severity, or asks an impossible question of them: 'Now, Katy — I won't let you leave the shop today, until you've bought me a big house. A big, big house! Can you buy me a big house?'

The child looks confused.

'No? You can't buy me a big house? Oh dear! Then I'll have to tell your mummy that you must stay here with me.'

The child, unable to discern the mock element in all this, crumbles inside and runs crying to their mother. Rosemary then chases after them: 'It's all right, you silly thing! I was only joking! Only joking!'

'Only joking!' It's a bleak mantra — the mantra of those who desire to hurt others, yet cannot take responsibility for their actions. They destroy trust — and then blame the victim; as if it is they who have misunderstood the situation. 'I was only joking!'

Why does Rosemary find it so hard to give happiness to a child? The psychology, I suppose, is not complex. She was not given happiness herself. What was taken from us when young, we will take from others; and what was not given to us, we will not give.

'It's all right, you silly thing! I was only joking! Only joking!'

These may be some of the worst words in the world.

Later, on the tills, as the queue dies down and there is time to think, I find myself looking up the meat aisle, and remembering another wide aisle – and the day I was ordained a priest in St Paul's Cathedral. It was a grand and self-important event, full of loud organ and lots of people in robes. I am particularly remembering afterwards, however, when as a newly ordained priest, I was leaving the building. Suddenly, there was a man on his knees, sliding towards me across the marble floor.

'A blessing, please, Father! Let me be the one to receive your first priestly blessing!'

I duly gave him my first priestly blessing, glad to be of service and all that, but learned later that mine was hardly the first he had received.

'He's a serial blessing-grabber, that one,' said the weary Cathedral verger.

'Ah!'

'Yeah – he slides from priest to priest like lard in a hot pan.'

I immediately regretted blessing his lunacy. Why had no one told him that he didn't need all this priestly nonsense; that he could save his sore knees; that all wonder and blessing was there inside him already? That believe it or not, and whisper it quietly – he could actually trust himself?

6.

THE CHILL GRIP OF POWER

In which Simon gets a surprise in the
cold store; Mohammed speaks of love
and Winston plays the philosopher. We
hear also of the 'Water Cooler Affair'.
We won't be drinking to that.

The day I was appointed chair of the shop union was the same day the Pope was elected. There the similarities end, however. For while his elevation took place beneath the fine art of the Sistine Chapel, with the mysterious white smoke rising, mine took place in the Cold Store, with nothing more mysterious than the bacon delivery and yesterday's waste.

'So, Si – it looks like the votes are pointing to you.'

This was a surprise.

'I didn't actually stand, Stav.'

'Let's just say your name was added to the mix.'

In order to protect itself from trade union interference, the store has developed its own internal union. It makes sense to them. The company have no interest in dealing with outside bodies when it comes to running their store. As it turned out, they had no interest in dealing with inside bodies either. But that was all in the future.

'So are you willing to take it on?' asks Stav. 'Big job obviously, but don't be scared – I'd support you in my capacity as management/union rep.'

In our store, there is one manager – Pinocchio – and four deputy managers. Stav is one of the deputies, but news that he'll be supporting me is something of a minus – like the current temperature. Stav is known for many things – his bonhomie, his jokes and his endless fag breaks. What he isn't known for is decisive action or the ability to handle conflict – and on the horizon, I could see the need for both.

'Could we talk somewhere warmer?' I ask.

'It's the only place available, mate.'

There was a moment as we talked when I genuinely feared for my life. Two members of staff interrupted my coronation, to collect the milk – and then took an age to sort out the dates on the cartons. Stav, keen to crack on, seemed to be considering a move into the adjoining freezer room. Certainly we'd not be disturbed there; we'd be dead, perhaps – but not disturbed. Fortunately, the milk collectors then left, and I accepted the post hurriedly.

I stepped out of that Cold Store as a man with a new role. I had gone in as one thing, and come out another, and I was taken back in time to when I first wore a dog collar in the street. I was then twenty-seven years old, and this was certainly a change. There I was, imagining that for the rest of my life, I must look intently into everyone's eyes – as one who really cared. It was a noble thought, but exhausting in practice; and in response to my earnest gaze, the public either checked to see their flies were done up, or looked on me with the sympathy reserved for those with special needs.

There were other changes as well. People started apologising for saying 'fuck' in my presence.

'S'cuse my French, Father!' they'd say.

Traditional blasphemy was fine. God! Christ! Jesus wept! They felt no need to backtrack on any of these. But 'fuck' was right out.

'S'cuse my French, Father!'

And here's a thing – old ladies would now open the door for me. 'Through you go, Father.'

I suppose without the dog collar, they'd expect me to be strong enough to open it myself.

No one's opening doors for me now, though, as I step back onto the shop floor. But there's a definite spring in my step, just like the Pope would have felt – if he'd been younger. I feel excited by my new job, and looking around the store, I enjoy a 'Moses Moment' – the moment when he gazed on his fellow Israelites in their hopeless Egyptian captivity: 'They have suffered for too long! I will gather these poor souls together, and we will stand as one against the whip-wielding management! Let my people go!'

Well, that was the idea, anyway.

Faith and Caspar are delighted by my appointment.

'We'll bring 'em down!' says Caspar confidently.

'You go for it, Si!' says Faith.

But that was about it with the applause.

Mohammed is my Bangladeshi colleague on the produce section, and we meet after work sometimes, for English lessons. (I'm giving them to him.) But he is not interested in my news – for he is currently in love, and things of the world can no longer hold him.

'I am in love, Simon!'

He is thirty years old, and new to England, but has been told by his family to get married. He has never had a girlfriend before, but last Saturday met a possible bride at a family get-together. It was mainly to allow the two sets of parents to meet each other, and Mohammed and the girl had not been allowed to meet alone. But a bit naughtily, they had secretly exchanged mobile phone numbers, and since then, had been running up large bills in love-struck conversation. I knew Mohammed was in love, because he was suddenly keen to do the nuts, as this was where the best reception was.

'I am in love, Simon! I have never known this feeling before. You cannot know how I feel!'

'I have been asked to be chair of the union,' I say determinedly.

'My heart is elsewhere, Simon. Truly, my heart is on higher things!'

He was beginning to sound like a cheap airport paperback. 'But I am happy for you,' he continues graciously. 'If that is what you want.'

I leave him checking for more texts from his beloved, and I go down to the tills. I find myself next to Winston and we work side by side for a while. He has heard about my appointment, and is determined to pour as much cold water on it as possible. And with Winston, that can be a lot of water.

'They still hold all the power, Simon,' he says, during a pause.

'Who's "they"?' I ask.

'The management, of course.'

'Power's in the imagination,' I say feistily. 'If you bestow power on yourself, then you have power. If you bestow power on another, then you don't. We have power if we believe in ourselves.'

'Power's in the wages,' he replies drily — and on one level, it's hard to argue. Sometimes I am overcome with money worries, and in that state, I am the least powerful person on earth. The worries come down like a mad fog, and leave me insane with fear. Yet still I am not at ease with his materialist view of power.

'So that's it, is it?' I ask.

'That which we cannot kill, we must bow to,' he says with a knowing look.

'I bow to no one.'

'Then, Simon – prepare to be killed. *Next!*'

Winston the philosopher is unnecessarily loud in his customer call. The shopper in question is about six feet from him, and blown away by the ferocity of his invitation. But the 'Next!' was aimed at me, not her. I felt like a worm – stamped on and gasping for breath.

🛒 🛒 🛒

All leaders have low moments – the period of history they don't really want mentioned. And the 'Water Cooler Affair' was undoubtedly mine. Like most things we set out to do or to be, it all began with such high hopes. With hindsight, however, I was too willing to trust the goodness of the people, and then displayed a lack of leadership when things began to go the way of the pear. Here is the tragic story.

As chair of the shop union, I had negotiated with the management for a water cooler in the canteen. The idea had arisen from our 'Suggestions Box'. This was an old shoe box, beautifully wrapped in brown paper by one of my colleagues, which served as a conduit both for staff frustration and creativity.

It wasn't always used in the cause of goodness and light. Occasionally, it became a manger for in-store vendettas, with poisonous notes about staff colleagues stuffed angrily inside. Generally, though, the box was used for the common good – as with the idea for a water cooler. After all, the bank down the road had one; my daughter told me there was one in the shop where she worked; and most significant of all, our canteen was not called 'The Black Hole' for nothing – being a windowless space, and unbearably hot in summer.

After much discussion, the store agreed to pay for the rent of the water cooler from the 'social fund', if the staff paid for the water itself. This seemed fair enough, and so we got on with things. The facility was installed, and the water tasted wonderful. Good times ahead surely? What possible cloud could appear in our bright blue sky?

Staff had the choice of whether to opt in to the chilled water. By signing up for it, they committed themselves to paying £2 each month. Twenty-five staff immediately said 'Yes' – for some were paying that amount daily for bottled water. It was really a very good deal all round; until it wasn't. And the worm began to turn when those who hadn't signed up for the water began to drink it anyway. The knowledge of their illicit activities proved corrosive.

Those who did pay began to resent paying. Why should they pay for water which other people were getting free? The water was being drunk at phenomenal rates, but the income was drying up. Rosemary probably used it the most, filling bottles from it. She was also the first one to refuse to pay.

A cloud of negativity began to gather round the venture. People started spying on others to see if they were 'secret drinkers'. And those I thought I could trust, I couldn't. Mohammed, someone I'd always supported, almost seemed to be willing the project to fail; for the union to fail; for me to fail.

'If others will not pay, then neither shall I,' he said, with some finality.

After two months of lovely chilled water in the canteen, we brought the experiment to an end. We are still trying to collect the money to pay off the final bill; and Rosemary has yet to pay anything at all.

Of course, I was disappointed by various people as the saga unravelled. But in the Water Cooler Affair, I am most disappointed with myself. I took the whole thing much too personally, for a start – and of course, these things are never personal. People hurt us from their unconscious pain. This was Jesus' thought when he hung on the cross and said rather surprisingly, 'Forgive them, Father – they know not what they do.' On one level, the Chief Priests et al knew exactly what they were doing – this execution had been well planned, and talked of for months, if not years. On another level, however, they hadn't a clue; they were acting unconsciously, from their own inadequacy and hurt. They were doing what they did, not because of who Jesus was, but because of who they were. It was not personal.

Secondly, my leadership was poor. I should have observed less, and intervened more. I should have gathered everyone together as soon as the rot set in, and asked: 'What's happening here? We have choices to make.'

The final straw for the water cooler revolution was when someone put salt in one of the water canisters, making a number of staff sick. Not all revolutions by the people are beautiful.

The day which started with my cold store coronation, closed with me stacking salads. They are prepared salads – chopped, washed, packed and ready for people who have no time. But I have time as I stack them – all the time in the world to reflect on some words Stav spoke earlier in the day: 'The thing is, Si, you won't be stupid; that's the thing. You've got more experience than the others. You know how things have to be.'

They were meant to be words of solidarity, binding me to the management's cause, but probably achieved the opposite. I thought back to Archbishop Romero in El Salvador. The corrupt government of the time appointed him because they thought he would toe the line. Romero was considered a conservative, a safe pair of hands; someone who knew how things had to be. But when Rutilio Grande, priest and personal friend, was murdered by the government, something inside Romero turned. From here on, he was no longer the silent conservative, the robed government puppet – instead, he began to speak out, home and abroad, against poverty, social injustice, assassination and torture in his country. In 1980, he too was assassinated – killed by a single shot to the heart, as he celebrated mass.

This is not El Salvador, as the expensive salads remind me; this is just a poorly run supermarket in London, England. But we do what we can where we are. Everyone's a leader somewhere, and nothing has to be. As leaders, whatever we have been, we now have choices to make.

7.

WAREHOUSE TERROR

In which Syed falls into a mysterious
sleep and Sapphy fears a haunting.
Meanwhile, mouse madness breaks out
— and a star guest makes a surprise
appearance.

Syed was fortunate not to be sacked. Had a manager other than Bryn been on duty, it is unlikely he would still be with us. To this day, he claims complete innocence, of course. This is what happened.

Sonny, our security guard, left the shop floor for a routine patrol of the warehouse. It is part of his brief to go there, to check for staff filching soft drinks or chocolate bars. But more pressing, Sonny just loves to remove himself from the troublesome shop floor — and does so as often as possible. The warehouse can only be reached by going up in the lift — or, by going round the back through the car park. But as Sonny rings the buzzer for the lift to be sent down, there is no reply. Someone must be there — but no one is answering. After a while, he decides to find Garry, and together they go round to the car park, to gain access through the back. This door is also locked, however, so they beat on it with a broom handle. Someone must be in there. What's going on? With no other means of access, and with Bryn in close attendance, they decide finally to break in.

'What else could we do?' he said. 'They could have been burglars!'

On arrival inside, however, they find no burglars – just Syed asleep on the floor. It is 11.00 am.

None of us are particularly surprised. Syed is a business student who studies through the night, and then sleeps during the day – whilst being paid. But now he has been caught comatose; Bryn stands over him, and he needs to think quickly. Bryn taps his prostrate form and asks what the fuck he is doing. Syed looks up: 'What happened?' he mumbles, rubbing his eyes and looking around in studied disbelief. 'What happened? I don't feel well.'

Bryn is in a dilemma. He wants to be a lad, and one of us – but he also wants to be our boss. He wants to have a good laugh; but he also wants to get angry. So which way will he jump – severity or mercy? Syed, meanwhile, maintains an attitude of complete incomprehension. He gets up off the floor and brushes himself down in a state of bewilderment, and for the rest of the shift claims to have no idea as to what left him dreaming on the warehouse floor.

'I don't know what happened. One moment I was getting some dry pasta down from the shelf, and then – blackout.'

It was, for him, a complete mystery. Only the carefully laid-out cardboard bed on which he rested spoke of something less mysterious.

But in choosing his bedroom, Syed chose well. The warehouse is the place to go when you've had enough. For a room with no books, it feels surprisingly like a library. It's calming and still, and I never mind a trip there.

'I wonder, young man – do you have any more of the cream biscuits?' asks a customer on the shop floor.

'Let me just go and check in the warehouse, madam.'

She thinks I'm being polite and helpful, but there are other agendas here. I'm just delighted to have reason to seek out the peace and tranquillity of the warehouse. And I may be gone some time.

Not everyone likes going there. Sapphy refuses to go there alone, because she's too frightened.

'Will you cum wiv me, Si?'

I agree to go up with her, and we share the lift. On arrival, I open the lift door, but she won't leave the lift and step into the warehouse until I have turned on the lights. And then she explains: 'Some people say ve warehahce is haun'ed, Si.'

I have heard this said, and the pipes can make unsettling noises. But haunted?

I have taken part in a few exorcisms in my time. It is surprising how many people with no connection to the Church give the local vicar a ring because of some perceived 'presence' in their home; rooms going suddenly cold, children unable to settle in the bedrooms or inexplicable smells appearing in the hallway. Sometimes it has serious financial ramifications – people unable to sell their house because of a sense of discomfort in those who look around. Whenever called, I would always say a prayer in the appropriate place, but was never gifted with any great sense of the 'other' – either present or departing. I would be a very average medium.

But there were more experienced exorcists than I, who saw the whole drama play out before them. I was with one such man when, in a large house, we chased a departed spirit from room to room, and then from floor to floor, until it was finally forced to leave by a window in the attic.

'Did you see it?' he asked when it was all over.

'No,' I replied.

'You didn't see it?'

'No.'

'You're joking?'

Funnily enough, I was going to ask him the same question. The exorcist himself was the most normal of men – but he saw abnormal things. Who knows what he would have found in our warehouse? Sapphy would not have been there to find out, however.

🛒 🛒 🛒

And while we're with the warehouse, I did find another stranger there recently, lying on the floor in the dark. And I blame Mohammed. If Mohammed hadn't mentioned the dead mouse in the chocolates, then none of this would have happened. But he did – and the consequence for the store was a bad outbreak of mouse madness.

'Vere's a mahce in ve ahhce!' screeched Sapphy one morning.

'A mouse in the house?' said Faith. 'I'm leaving. Health and safety.'

One of the first signs of mouse madness is a belief that they are everywhere. Each step is checked to make sure there are no vermin beneath your feet; while each sudden movement is a rodent running for cover. Sightings become commonplace, with the hysteria comparable to the 1970s when it was really very hard to go shopping without encountering at least two UFOs and one alien life form. Today, however, it's encounters of the mouse kind, and Sapphy is the worst.

'Aagghh!'

I hear the scream, and run into the canteen. Sapphy is on a chair, with her hands held up in terror.

'I saw one! I swear I saw it!'

'Where?'

'It ran over vere!'

'What – behind the fridge?'

'Yeah – I fink so. Ve're so quick! It was like a blur. Almost like it weren't vere!'

I get a bit jittery around mice myself, but in the face of Sapphy's hysteria, I become as calm as the Dead Sea. I look at Sapphy standing on a chair, terrorised by a fictitious blur. It's a shame we spend so much time in fear of things that don't exist, but there we are. In the meantime, I stay with Sapphy and her madness until she feels safe to come down. Her trauma recovery is not helped by the arrival of Caspar.

'I'm not going back into the warehouse,' he says.

'What do you mean?'

'I saw a mouse.'

'In the warehouse?'

'Yep.'

'Are you sure?'

'You can't be sure – they're so quick.'

'Vat's juzz what I said,' says Sapphy. 'They're such quick li'al bleed-arz – you don't actually see 'em!'

'It's almost like they're not there,' I say, interrupting Hallucinators Anonymous.

'That's right,' says Caspar, missing the point.

'I saw one in the cann-een!'

'You saw one in the canteen?' says Caspar. 'Looks like they're everywhere then.' He sounds like a President informed of wide-spread terrorist infiltration of the CIA.

'Have you seen our new special offer?' asks Garry as he joins us. 'Tread on one, get one free.'

Sapphy and Caspar are not laughing.

'We nee' to get a man in to kill 'em,' says Sapphy.

And that's what we did. The following Tuesday, the Pest Control Officer is lying on the floor of the warehouse, in the dark. My first thought is that it's a dead body.

'Hello?' I call out, my voice betraying slight fear.

'Don't mind me!' says the dead body. 'Come on in!'

So the figure on the floor is alive – and speaks with a lyrical Welsh accent.

'Can you not find the light switch?' I ask.

He wouldn't be the first to spend a dark couple of hours looking for it. However, it turns out the darkness is planned. Yesterday, he had put down some luminous tracking dust.

'Just taking a look at the extent of the problem,' he says.

'And?'

'Well, I don't see any problem at all, to be perfectly honest with you. There are no trails to be seen.'

'You mean we don't have mice?'

He gets up off the floor, picks up his cup of tea, and suddenly acquires a professorial tone: 'The house mouse is the most common mammal in the cities, with black rod-shaped droppings of between three and six millimetres, and quite prolific powers of urination.'

'Really?'

'They can enter a property through holes as small as five millimetres, generally gaining access through air bricks or air vents, and as I say – real Olympic pissers.'

'Everyone's good at something.'

'Oh, I'll tell you what they're really good at, boyo – transmitting disease!'

'Really? I didn't have them down as disease merchants.'

'The common mouse promotes more disease than a hospital ward! Salmonellosis, rickettsialpox, tapeworm, ratbite fever, lymphocytic choriomeningitis – how's that to be going along with?!'

Mervyn the Mouse Man knew more about mice than was either legal, decent – or indeed, interesting. There's a thin line between being passionate about a subject and ever so slightly dull.

'But there's no mice here,' he added, with some disappointment. 'And I was told you had an infestation.'

'I think it was more an infestation of the mind.'

'You can never be absolutely sure,' he said, finishing his tea. 'And if they aren't here today, they'll be along tomorrow.'

'There's a cheering thought.'

'And they'll gnaw through wood to get to food if they need to!'

'Can I turn the light on now?' I ask, trying to bring the lecture to a close. 'I've been sent up here to find some cat food.'

'You and me alike!' quipped Mervyn, really quite tickled by the comedy of it all.

I am glad when finally Mervyn takes the lift down and leaves me alone with the warehouse. It has always been a place of sanctuary for me; and never a place for talking. I listen again to my breathing, which is a way of reminding myself who I am. Perhaps this is a definition of a holy place – somewhere that reminds us who we are.

I remember years ago running a church and community centre in the heart of London. It was a good place, full of activity; but I was concerned we had no quiet place amidst it all. So we raised some money, took an old room that was used for everything and nothing, brought in architects, builders, carpenters and artists – and created a beautiful prayer chapel; a place where anyone could step in off the street and remember who they were.

The opening was particularly remembered.

It had been a real problem finding someone to open the chapel. After all, we were hardly a glamorous venue, set as we were in some of the poorer backstreets of the capital. Rejection letters from politicians and celebrities flooded in; they were all so eager to be with us, yet sadly so busy. I remember being turned down not just by the Minister for the Environment, but also by his Private Secretary – and we hadn't even asked him. We were thinking of cancelling the idea of a big opening when a letter arrived from Buckingham Palace, saying that the Queen would be most interested in coming to open our Prayer Chapel – if that was all right with us. We thought it was a joke at first, but four months later, she did – the Queen came to open our Prayer Chapel, along with half the world's media. It was a little embarrassing in a way, because it was, in essence, only a converted room. But what a room! And what a day – the day the Queen came!

In the meantime, however, with Mervyn the Mouse Man gone, I locate the cat food hidden behind a stack of bleach. I return to the shop floor. Mervyn is now in the canteen, regaling eager listeners with tales of derring-do in the pest control world. He is the Indiana Jones of vermin adventures, with a rat story for every occasion. The audience is agog.

'Is it true that mice, unlike rats, don't actually need a water supply?' asked Winston, fresh from an evening with the UK Discovery channel. 'That they get the liquid they need from their food?'

'It is indeed true, my friend. Mice have no need of a water supply. And I'll tell you another thing, boyo…'

They hang on his every word. It's strange how fascinated we are by the things we fear and loathe – and how bored we are by the things we say we love.

8.

MY FRIEND AND ENEMY MOHAMMED

In which Mohammed considers both his immigrant future and the challenge of regular sex. Simon, meanwhile, is both seduced by power and humiliated by rejection — and a big international darts match takes place. Sports reporting at its finest.

Mohammed is my friend, who now works the produce aisle with me. He used to work the meat aisle, but as they say, life is change. Who knows what's round the corner? The deli section? Desserts? Household goods? Everyone's got a dream.

He was born in Bangladesh, where his father was a government official, and he a university graduate in chemistry. They had two servants in their house, which meant that when he came to this country two years ago, he had never actually washed up. In his country, manual labour would have been entirely inappropriate for one of his class. In England, however, he is just another Asian shop worker, dreaming of the next step up from the minimum wage.

He has an excellent grasp of written English. He read English novels in Bangladesh, and continues to do so here.

He likes the science fiction sagas of other worlds – worlds other than England. His spoken English lags behind, however, and he is not easy to understand. He gets frustrated by this, and we spend much time on pronunciation classes as we stack the shelves. I will say the word, and then he will try and copy me. But he can't. Every nation's mouth is designed to make different noises, and sometimes it's too late to change.

'I will never get a job,' he says in despair.

'You've got a job,' I say.

'A good job – I will not get a good job. I know people cannot understand what I say.'

This is true. He often has to send customers to me, when he can't understand what they are saying, or if they can't understand him. He believes he is worth more than this, and wants a good job. He'd been offered a bank post recently, by an Asian friend – but they couldn't take him on because of his visa situation.

I myself have been planning a move to London Transport, with Mohammed and another member of staff. The lowest rung of the LT ladder still pays twice as much as the supermarket – and you get free travel. In preparation, I helped the other two with their CVs and coached them for the interview. But here's the thing – when we heard back from LT, although they were both given interviews, I was not.

'Dear Mr Parke, Thank you for your application to LT,' they say in their letter. 'Unfortunately, we do not believe you currently possess the right qualifications.'

I'm fifty, educated, running fit, and with a lifetime's experience of people. But I apparently do not possess the right qualifications to collect tickets and help people find the Northern Line. LT do then add, however, that 'with more experience, I could yet be considered, some time in the future'.

More experience in what, I wonder? Fly fishing? Spoon bending? Carpet weaving? If it wasn't happening to me, I'd be laughing. Instead, I feel strangely humiliated, especially as Mohammed seems to gain a measure of pleasure from my failure.

'Perhaps you should do as they say,' he says casually, 'gain more experience.'

Everyone's trying to leave this place, of course. In our minds, it's a corridor, not a room – a place we are passing through. Perhaps we will get a job on the railways or in a beauty salon or in a bank. We were going to leave last year, and we are going to leave this year. It is likely we will also be leaving next year.

I am aware of the shock, and sometimes embarrassment, of those who knew me as a vicar – and now find me serving them behind a till. I tell them that I'm happy, but I'm not sure they believe me.

'I hope it all works out,' they say.

'It is working out.'

'Yeah – but you know what I mean. Something better, and all that.'

'I trust the pavement I walk on.'

'I didn't realise you'd come to this until Dave Roberts mentioned it. But good luck, Father. We miss you and your dog.'

🛒 🛒 🛒

I have spoken of Mohammed's love life, which was slow to start – but accelerated, and then threw him into a great panic. His first relationship I have already mentioned. It lasted a week and was a sandwich of two brief meetings, and a week of furious texting in between. It came to an end when the families decided against it — leaving Mohammed to decide against it, in his own time. He fell out of love as quickly as he had fallen into it, and waited for the next woman to be presented to him. And soon she was, one Saturday afternoon in Wolverhampton — he was in love again.

'I am definitely in love, Simon.'

'You met her?'

'I met her.'

'And did you talk?'

'A little — but her sisters were there too. They were nice. But they would not leave us alone.'

In the tradition of the arranged marriage, the two individuals should not communicate privately during the protracted business of family negotiations. In former times, this was not hard to enforce. You just kept them apart until the deal was done. But the mobile phone has blown that tradition out of the water.

'We spoke for seven hours last night!' Mohammed tells me.

I find him on the phone again today, by the nuts. This conversation is forbidden both by the store and by his family — but he cannot help himself. His lack of sleep leaves him lost and languid on the shop floor, but what can he do? He is in love, or at least he thinks he is, for he has only one other relationship to compare it with, and that was largely conducted by text like this one. Again, he has only met this woman once, but he is quite overwhelmed:

'I am overwhelmed! I think of her all the time, Simon! Oh my God! All the time.'

Well, time passes and marriage is definitely on the cards. With the reality of marriage looming, Mohammed starts to get worried.

'Is it true you have to make love five times a day?' he asks me, as we put out the organic chickens.

I don't know who has told him this, but it's a concern. He has never made love once, so five times a day is certainly a step up. As he reflects on the challenge, however, he becomes bold in the face of fear.

'I could do that,' he says, before I can reply. 'No problem. I will go back at lunchtimes.'

I will shortly reveal the result of the first ever international darts tournament between England and Bangladesh, because I don't suppose you saw it on television. But for the moment, I am putting out the fruit juices, and Mohammed is pressing me. He won't let the matter rest.

'You should be a coach, Simon.'

Mohammed and I were to be made coaches together. They are a new idea, and there are to be six in the store. They will be paid a little more than the others – about £7.00 an hour. They will train newcomers in the fine arts of shelf stacking and till work, and jump when the managers say 'Jump'. When the managers are ensconced in the office with their sandwiches and chips, it is coaches who will give the orders on the shop floor.

I had pulled out of the process, however. I would have liked the extra pay, but found myself too old and too arrogant to be a mouthpiece for management monkeys. I find it hard to give orders I do believe in, let alone orders I don't. The managers are angry at my opt-out. They had, after all, thrown a lifeline to this loser in life, and might have expected me to be grateful. For good or ill, however, I just can't dance to their tune.

Mohammed is not pleased and hunts me down.

'You should be a coach, Simon.'

'No – I think it might be best if I keep out of it.'

'There is still time to change your mind.'

'Maybe.'

I must admit, I am still wavering. I have never experienced promotion in my life, and feel myself seduced. Vaulting ambition intoxicates my blood, and excites my tired veins. Someone is actually offering me promotion! More than that, I was the first person they asked, and this wonderfully tickles my pride.

'So you will consider it?' asks Mohammed.

'I've said "No". I'll probably stick with that.'

'But I have spoken to the management.'

'What do they say?'

'They say it is your decision.'

'Yes, well that's true.'

'No! What the fuck! I will decide for you! You will become a coach. We will change the shop together. We will take them on!'

I like the cut of his jib, and I have to say that as we talk, I nearly change my mind – I really do. *Nearly* – but not quite.

Mohammed would like to buy a house, but currently lives on a rickety staircase above a Bangladeshi restaurant. I recently went round to his rickety staircase for a meal. We were joined by a lawyer from Bangladesh, who now cleans and serves in a large hotel. He also lives on the rickety staircase, and his truly appalling wages make Mohammed and me feel very rich.

Mohammed's generosity shames me. We eat lamb and rice, and he buys my favourite drink which is Barley Wine. In fact, he buys so much of it that I have to take some home, as he won't touch it. He is more of a Blue Nun man – though is thinking of returning to the alcohol-free life of the faithful Muslim. (He has been unfaithful for a few years now.)

Sensing danger, I am careful with the spicy sauce. He says it isn't spicy at all, until the alcohol starts on him like a truth drug.

'A little spicy, perhaps,' he concedes.

He smokes his way through the evening. We struggle a bit with dialogue, as his lawyer friend's English is much worse than Mohammed's, and my Bangla worse still. So the evening is a linguistic compromise between Bangla and English, but closes with a game of darts that transcends language barriers. Mohammed has a dartboard on the wall, but due to lack of space, you have to stand with one leg on the chair in order to throw, which makes things a good deal trickier. The large halo of indentations in the wall around the board reveals just how tricky.

Mohammed has taken to darts. It is a western game and not deeply embedded in Bangladeshi culture. 'One hundred and eighty!' is not often heard in the teahouses of Dhaka. (It isn't much heard on this particular evening either. More like 'Eighteen!' or 'One!') But for Mohammed, it is a fine game: cheap, suitable for small spaces and sociable. And Mohammed, starting from the bottom in a strange land, is a most sociable person.

He is not sociable when talking about politics, of course. Two things I have learned in life: first, there is no happy outcome to the board game Monopoly. And second, there is no happy outcome from a political discussion with Mohammed. He is just too angry. Wherever the discussion starts – and often it was just me asking questions – it would end with rage at oppressors who had reduced his country to its present state. The British were deemed the worst; with India coming up on the outside, as the new colonial power. We may be putting out lovely strawberries together, on a bright summer's day – but anger with the actions of the British Empire one hundred years ago is transferred instantly onto me.

'It is too late. What's done is done. There is no hope for my country.'

I have learned not to ask questions about his homeland as we put out the strawberries.

Neither is he sociable during Ramadan. His blood sugar is low due to the fast, and this is not good news for anyone. He is listless on the shop floor, and slightly grumpy – if it's a spiritual experience, it's well disguised. I remember when I used to fast for twenty-four hours every week. I was told it would take me to new levels of holiness, but I am not sure the pay-off is quite that simple. Certainly it is hard to be joyful during this time, and there is no question that our Muslim brothers and sisters struggle at work, all sullen and slow around the aisles. Even though the time changes daily, they know the exact minute of each evening when they will be able to eat and drink again. Ramadan ends with Eid, and then Mohammed is back to his best. I remember his first words to me with a full belly after last year's Eid celebrations:

'Now we will fuck the management!' he declared.

Enlightenment.

Meanwhile, getting back to the sports news – because

really, what else is there? – I am both happy and proud to report that in the first official Bangladesh vs England darts tournament, England came from behind (the chair) to win. And until the result became clear, the match was played in a good spirit.

9.

BUY NONE – GET ONE FREE!

In which Sonny doesn't get his man, but
Simon does – along with a right
telling-off. If looks could kill!
Meanwhile, the whistle blower
unsettles Pinocchio; Sonny has therapy;
a thief claims his rights, and there's a
surprise hug and a kiss for
you-know-who.

We have a security guard in the store, but that's not the same as having security. How so?

Sonny our security guard starts his shift at 2.00 pm, and gets on with everyone. There is no one Sonny doesn't get on with. Do not be fooled by his job title, however. He is a nice man, who plays a full part in shop life – but he doesn't catch thieves; indeed, he hates all conflict. I'm not sure who advised him towards his current employment.

The company employs security staff reluctantly, and we only qualify for eight hours during the day. This means that in the morning, we must watch the store for ourselves. As shop floor staff, we are encouraged to be vigilant. But beyond this, things get a little vague. In my early days with the store, I was naïve enough to imagine that thieves should be chased and apprehended. Twice I chased thieves down the road and caught them. I run every morning, including a half marathon every Sunday, so truly, it was a joy to be out of the shop, feeling the breeze, and with a runner ahead of me to follow.

I chased the first bloke for about 300 yards and he was understandably put out by my arrival on his shoulder. He had sprinted out of the shop, crossed the road, and then disappeared at speed down a side street. I saw him through the window, heard Faith screaming 'Thief!' and thought 'Why not?' I am almost run over myself as I leg it across the road, aware that he has a start on me. But a couple of hundred fast yards later, I turn the corner to find him meandering along, contemplating his free salmon lunch.

He is most perturbed when I join him, and I can see his point of view. People didn't usually come after him when he stole things, and we all find it hard when our patterns are disrupted.

'I'll fucking stab you,' he says, as a way of moving me on.

But he seemed an unlikely stabber, and so we walked together for a while. He asks me if I'd worked in the shop long, and I am just beginning my answer when he drops the fish at my feet and runs off. It was an all too brief encounter, and I'm ashamed to say I haven't kept in touch.

The second thief was a middle-aged man and a physical wreck, who unwisely chose to escape up the hill with his £100 worth of meat. He had filled his basket with prime steaks, moved towards the tills as if to pay, and then suddenly made for the door. He pushed past me, so I was after him immediately, and it proved a disappointingly short chase. It was like watching a man run up a sand dune, and he dropped the meat about a hundred yards from the store, breathless. Mohammed joined me as we watched him stagger off towards the flats. I was a bit worried for his health as he disappeared from view; he didn't look well, and some steak might have done him good. But there we are. If you don't have a getaway driver, you need to be in shape for stunts like this. At least next time he should consider a downhill escape.

If I had been expecting applause, however, I was to be disappointed. On both occasions, the managers were furious, and disciplinary action was considered.

'What were you doing, Si?'

'I was catching a thief.'

'Yeah, but you don't.'

'Why not? They're thieves.'

'That may be, but you're not insured to go off the premises.'

'I didn't know you cared.'

'It's not worth the risk for thirty quid's worth of salmon.'

'So what am I supposed to do?'

'Stay vigilant, of course.'

'Stay vigilant?'

'Yeah – you know, keep your eyes open and all that.'

'Keep my eyes open as they run past me out of the door?'

'You can't chase them, Si.'

'So staff must be vigilant at all times and then promptly do nothing.'

'Chase anyone again, Si, and you'll be sacked. No – I mean it. I'll have no choice.'

And this I have since tried to do. I diligently do nothing as they saunter out with their wine. Or cheese. One thief, unknown to anyone, was gradually removing our entire cheese section. He was taking as much as he could reasonably carry, dumping it behind a hedge up the road, and then returning for more. In the end, a customer noticed this strange but developing pile of dairy products, and the thief was caught – though nothing was done.

And being vigilant and doing nothing is very much Sonny's stock-in-trade – if we remove vigilance from the equation. He is a Buddhist from Sri Lanka and reminds me of an English Buddhist security guard I used to work with in another store. He would not step on a snail or swat a fly; he was unlikely, therefore, to disturb a shoplifter. He wasn't pro-shoplifting as such; he just believed in 'live and let steal'. After all, there are no such things as 'possessions' in the end.

Sonny is the same – opposed to the catching of thieves, though more through personality than religion. His greatest fear in life is conflict. It makes him feel extremely uncomfortable. Were he in therapy, it would not be long before this one came up: 'So tell me, Sonny? What is it about conflict that so frightens you? And why is it that you go to such lengths to avoid it?'

But Sonny is not in therapy. He is a security guard on the shop floor, trying to avoid thieves because he knows if he finds one, he may have to do something. He has developed strategies however. If he has to follow a thief, he will do so from the back of the shop. This means that if they make a break for it towards the door, they will have a free run, without having to encounter him. He has never caught a thief in his time in the store.

He has other talents, of course. He is diligent in collecting baskets from behind the tills; he helps customers with their shopping, advises them about desserts and checks the shelves for items past their sell-by date. Sometimes he will visit my produce section, and present me with an out-of-date mango.

'It is not good, Simon,' he says, in the manner of a disappointed father speaking to his wayward son.

This is true; it is not good. But then I've caught two more thieves than him, which isn't good either.

🛒 🛒 🛒

The shop wants security — and so pays for eight hours — but more than that, it doesn't want a fuss. It wants staff to be vigilant — and then to do nothing. We don't want a scene. That's the worst thing — a scene! Oooh la la! Which is why Pinocchio turns down the whistle idea.

'People are routinely taking wine from the store,' I say in a union meeting. 'And Faith has had this idea about a whistle.'

'A whistle?' asks Pinocchio nervously. 'How do you mean?'

'Faith sees thieves before anyone. She's down there on the till, with clear views of the aisles. She sees them; knows who they are.'

'Well, she should tell a manager.'

'How about she just blows a whistle, to alert other staff?'

'She doesn't need to blow a whistle. She just needs to tell a manager.'

'If she can find one — you're normally hiding out the back.'

'There's always a manager around.'

'Untrue.'

'It's the proper procedure.'

'What?' says Caspar. 'So Faith leaves the till, walks the length of the store, out the back, down to the office, to find a manager, who may or may not come when asked?'

'By which time the thief is long gone,' adds Garry.

'I'm sorry — but that isn't a security system.'

'I don't think a whistle is appropriate,' says Pinocchio. 'Who wants a whistle blowing on the shop floor?'

'I've never seen a customer sad to see a thief caught,' I say.

'It's entertainment, isn't it?' says Garry.

'It's fucking justice,' says Caspar.

'Well, I will consider the whistle idea,' says Pinocchio, but he never does, because he doesn't want a scene. More than security, he wants to avoid a scene, which is why we had that ridiculous business with the thief threatening to take us to court.

Faith had eventually got frustrated. Every day, she watched the thieves come in; she watched them thieve and then she watched them leave. She has three children, spends more than she should, lives more in the red than the black – but doesn't steal.

'It's not right,' she says.

And then one day, it just slips out. As one of the regulars walks past her towards the door, she says, 'You're a thief.'

Oh, the upset and indignation!

'What did you call me?'

'You heard what I said,' says Faith.

He moves towards her threateningly, and other staff quickly move to protect her.

A raised voice! An unseemly incident! A scene! Pinocchio is quickly there, to calm things. Faith is asked to apologise, but she refuses.

'I ain't apologising to him.'

'I demand an apology,' says the thief.

'Search him,' says Faith.

'I want an apology, or I'm going to the police,' says the thief. Well, that's a joke.

'I quite understand, sir,' says Pinocchio, as I take Faith away.

He is with the indignant thief for some time, wading deep in absurdity. He nods his head in agreement and professional shame as the man's tragic story of mistaken identity is told.

He is no thief and is furious to be so called! He wants her sacked! It is an infringement of his human rights, and could end up in the European Courts! etc etc. Pinocchio just wants him off the premises.

'Please don't make any more of a scene!' he is thinking. 'I'll toady, be craven, grovel and sell Faith down the river – I'll do anything as long as you promise to go! But no more scenes – supermarkets hate scenes!'

I can't bear to watch this capitulation. Later, Pinocchio pulls Faith in to say that there's not much he can do if the man carries out his threat to report her to Head Office.

'Did you search him?' she asks.

'It was hardly the time or the place!' says Pinocchio, with an amused 'Right! Like that was appropriate!' tone to his voice.

🛒 🛒 🛒

Like the store, I too want security – but do I really? I had security in the Church, but walked away from it. Perhaps I want the search more – the search that is free from an institution's kind binding. So I walked from security. And yet when a friend and former parishioner drops in this afternoon to do some shopping, suddenly I am talking about money and almost crying. How the priest has fallen! Crying on the shop floor in economic fear.

I think of the story of the old man who lives in a cave on a hillside, with only one possession – a table. One night the old man is woken by a thief who has come for the table.

'I am sorry it is so little,' he says. 'It is a beautiful moon tonight, and if I could give that to you, then truly I would!'

But I am not the old man on the hill, as I stand tearful by the chiller cabinets. Instead, I am overwhelmed by a wave of insecurity crashing across my psyche; survival fears flood me, because I'm wondering what I'm going to do for the rest of my life, and wondering how I'll survive, and thinking that although most days I get up and know I'm the luckiest man in the world, this afternoon I am overwhelmed with self-pity, and feeling the unluckiest of all.

My friend listens kindly, but what can she do? What can anyone do with someone else's version of hell?

'If the doors of perception were cleansed,' says William Blake, 'everything would appear to man as it is – infinite. For man has closed himself up, until he sees all things through the narrow chinks of his cavern.'

So my friend stays to listen; she listens to the madman, who sees only through his narrow chinks – and then goes off to do her shopping. I'm left feeling a bit of a fool, and return to the shelves, filling, and filling again. In a while, my friend surprises me, returning to place a bar of Swiss chocolate in my hand.

'Don't worry,' she says. 'I have paid for it.'

'I won't chase you then.'

'I wouldn't mind.'

'Nor would I!'

She then gives me a hug and a kiss, and leaves. It's a sort of security.

10.

IT'S TRUE — GOD IS IN THE RETAIL

In which Simon gets Jehovah'd and
Rosemary denounces the Big Bang.
Bryn gets a holiday request he can't
turn down — on religious grounds;
Brian discovers he has demonic powers,
and the canteen becomes a truth
market, with many different sellers.

Someone called supermarkets the new temples of the secular society — and this would be a good description of them, if they weren't so full of religion.

On the staff here, we have every belief under the sun, and at least one person that worships it. I am presently trapped in a conversation with Rosemary, our Jehovah's Witness from Ghana — and the one who makes children cry.

'She could make an onion cry,' said Caspar the other day. He doesn't run her Fan Club.

Rosemary also reckons all men are disgusting because they only want one thing.

'I see men looking,' she says, with a curl of her full and glossy lips and a wave of her many-ringed fingers. 'They only want one thing.'

'Fish and chips?'

'You know what I mean, Si!' she says, flirtatiously.

'Get behind me, Rosemary. You're leading me astray.'

'Huh!'

I'm aware that Rosemary only wants one thing, but she may be right about men as well. In the meantime, she walks down the aisles of the store like a catwalk model, conscious of her every move. She is glam, disdainful, and just over five feet tall.

She isn't popular amongst the staff. Caspar calls her 'the Poison Dwarf', because, as he says, 'she's short and poisonous'. She schemes constantly, and displays a remarkable capacity to alienate people, manipulate people or simply leave them speechless with frustration. She wants eventually to go into Human Resources.

She has recently decided she likes me, after initially deciding she hated me. She was all over someone else, but now she's all over me. What heralded the change? Who knows? But the fact is, last week she came and sat on my lap during a team briefing, and said quite out of the blue as we walked past the cakes that she would like to meet my father.

Things are about to take a turn for the worse, however, for I am about to be, well – 'Jehovah'd'.

It all starts innocently enough, as we chat about this and that.

'Ninety-eight per cent of my country go to church,' she declares.

They are back with corruption on Monday, of course, because life is hard, with or without God.

'And the education is better in Ghana. My school in Accra was way better than any here. I studied *Jane Eyre*, *Coriolanus* and *Hard Times* for A level.'

Soon, however, courtesy of Rosemary, my own hard times come to call, as I ask her to guess what vegetable I'm holding.

'I don't know, Si,' she says. 'Tell me.'

'It's fennel,' I say.

'Isn't that amazing,' she says.

'Well, I suppose so – moderately amazing, anyway.'

I wasn't over the moon about the fennel. It had charm, but wasn't the Grand Canyon or anything. It was banter, nothing more.

'So many different vegetables!' continues Rosemary, and it is at this moment I sense the nightmare to come.

'Right,' I say, uneasily.

'Did you know there are over five thousand types of apple, for instance – five thousand, Simon!'

'Really?'

'Probably more, in fact.'

This is nonsense, but I see where it is leading.

'We think we know it all,' she continues, 'and then we go and discover another piece of God's amazing creation. And yet some people still talk about the Big Bang. Huh!' From fennel to creationism in twenty seconds – you have to admire her skill. I ask about the possibility of God creating the world through the Big Bang.

'I mean, does it matter exactly how God created the world?'

'It matters a great deal, Simon.'

'Oh.'

'The Big Bang cannot be true, because the Bible says that God is an orderly God.'

'I don't remember that bit,' I say, quite unable to recall anything orderly in the Bible. Floods? Plagues? Massacres? Stables? Mad pigs leaping over cliffs? Temple tables overturned? Crucifixions? The apocalypse? I'm struggling to see the order.

She grabs me in both a persuasive and sexual way, and tells

me that I would see God was orderly if I opened my eyes. She then lets go of me, and we talk a little more about Big Bangs, until finally I manage to get back to my fennel. I am angry and unsettled, feeling slightly mugged by religion. Rosemary is angry and unsettled too. There may be 5,000 wonderful varieties of apple, but she is fucking furious I have rejected her religious advances. She does not acknowledge me for the rest of the day. Religion can be a divisive little fellow.

🛒 🛒 🛒

But religion can also wield power, as a recent holiday request showed.

'Er, I was wondering about these holiday dates for August,' says Brian to Bryn. Brian is not too hopeful as he is late with his request, and everyone wants August for their holidays.

'They'll be fine, Brian,' says Bryn.

'But you haven't seen them yet.'

'No worries.'

No worries? There's normally a frustrating three-week wait before you hear.

'I know certain other individuals have had difficulty with August dates.'

'They'll be fine, Brian,' says Bryn. 'Let me see. Yep, fine. Leave them to me.'

Brian gets the holidays he wants because he is a witch. We will hear more about him later, but that is the key fact now. Brian is a self-confessed witch, and Bryn is just a little bit scared of being cursed.

Part of him dismisses the whole witch thing as a load of baloney, of course:

'It's fucking nonsense!' he says, with laddish confidence.

But then again, why risk being cursed and joining the undead, just for a holiday request? Give it to him — might as well.

Bryn's fear is misplaced, because although Brian is a witch, he is an honourable man. He may leave magazines like *New Pagan* and *Norse Gods Monthly* in the canteen, and wear a spooky black fedora hat in the street — but who does it hurt? Can he walk through glass, though? This was a big issue for a while. Sapphy and Caspar believed he could, as they once saw him walk through the shop's locked front door without opening it. Sapphy was doing the strawberries at the time by the entrance, when she saw Brian outside — and then suddenly he was inside!

'Ee were art-sii — ven suddenly, ee were insii!' said Sapphy. 'My life — it were well scary!'

'I tell you, Si,' said Caspar, conspiratorially: 'That man can walk through doors.'

After this, some ascribed demonic powers to Brian, who did not seem displeased. He was happy with any sort of fame. Caspar can pull the girls, which Brian struggles with. But Brian can walk through glass doors — so who is better off?

But let us not get hysterical. Sure, Brian wears his trousers halfway up his chest. And when his flies are undone — as often they are — his beige company shirt dangles through them in an unfortunate fashion, causing at least one customer to scream. But we'll keep calm. This isn't *The Return of the Zombies Part 4*! Brian is simply a white witch, who goes to Stonehenge on the Summer Solstice; uses Halloween to reflect on his own mortality, and generally feels angry that Christianity has stolen all the pagan festivals. As for the glass door incident, a fault explained all. Even when set on 'closed', the door would open if pushed in the right place; and Brian knew the right place.

He does live on high caffeine drinks for the first half hour in the store. This is less about being a witch, though; and more about waking up, which he finds hard.

'It definitely has a speedening effect,' he says, as another can is poured down his throat.

God help us when he forgets it, then – because even when energised, he moves like a slug with cramp. No offence.

🛒 🛒 🛒

When things are going well, religion really doesn't matter; when people relate happily as humans, centuries of theological thuggery don't mean a thing. Our various religions may all be murdering each other around the world, but in the store, while personal relations are good, all is peace and calm. 'When the shoe fits, the foot is forgotten,' as they say. It's only when things go wrong that attitudes change, and the worm turns. When there's tension in the air, suddenly religion becomes important.

'What religion is Rosemary?' asks Mohammed, who has grown to hate her.

'She's a Jehovah's Witness,' I say.

'A what?'

'A Jehovah's Witness. You may not have heard of them.'

I wasn't sure how big they were in Bangladesh.

'Whatever her religion, it's shit,' he says.

It is more a comment on Rosemary than her particular faith; but in tense times, the two become linked, and difference becomes an issue.

🛒 🛒 🛒

And of course with so many religions around, the canteen sometimes resembles a truth market, everyone pitching their wares. We have Sonny the Buddhist, Mohammed the Muslim, Sapphy the Christian, Brian the Witch, Winston the atheist, Rosemary the Jehovah's Witness and Vinnith the Hindu. These things don't matter when you are stood together on the till, or putting out the satsumas. But if one seller in the truth market starts pitching, others join in. And today, it is Sonny who makes his pitch first:

'Buddhism is the oldest and the wisest,' says Sonny.

'Islam is the final revelation,' says Mohammed.

'Yeah – but what abow Jesus?' asks Sapphy.

'Jesus was a thief,' says Brian, 'or at least his followers are, taking other people's festivals!'

'Jesus was not a thief.'

'He was a prophet,' says Mohammed, 'but not the ultimate prophet.'

'It's all stuff and nonsense,' says Winston. 'I don't know why any of you bother.'

'I like the many gods of Hinduism,' says Vinnith. 'I've known them from childhood.'

'I've known eczema from childhood,' says Winston. 'Doesn't mean I want to keep it.'

'You are a sad man, if you do not have God,' says Rosemary, adding quickly, 'the true God, that is.'

'Well, you can't all be right!' says Caspar in some frustration, because he'd been wanting answers.

'But we all think we are,' says Winston. 'And that's how we'll die – deluded until the last.'

'Anyone for tennis?' asks Garry.

'What do you think, Si?' asks Sapphy later, when the queue on the tills finally disappears. 'You didn't join in our li'al religious debate at lunch.'

'Religious debate is as useful as strangling jelly.'

'Bit surprisin' for someone who were a priest!'

'Not really – it's just meaningless, that's all.'

'I find it orr quii intrestin'.'

'"When the heart is good, 'for' and 'against' – these things are forgotten." I prefer a good heart to a good debate.'

'I've only ever known the Greek Orfodox stuff, me. Greek Orfodox, I am – born and bred!'

'Well, there are worse places to start.'

'Yeah, no one will change me. No one – though I doan really believe any of it.'

11.

FREEZE!
YOU'RE NICKED!

In which management get over-excited,
and two of the staff get handcuffed!
Meanwhile, Stav calls me into the
office on a matter of some urgency,
Sapphy has money worries, Bryn gets
distracted — and the whodunnit
is finally solved.

There is an atmosphere of intense excitement in the store today, on this damp Monday morning. On opening up, Garry and I are met not by one manager — but three! Three managers in at 6.30 am?

'A parallel universe!' says Garry.

But they are on too much of a high to notice our astonishment. They are happy to be early, and up for all that lies ahead.

On a normal day, if a manager is in by 6.30 then, well, hallelujah — but they'll probably be snug in the office with yesterday's figures, or moodily surveying staffing sheets. But not today — no way! These young turks of the retail trade are experiencing the adrenaline rush of white water rafting. For once, they won't be spending their working hours answering old ladies' queries about the disappointing range of custards.

Instead, they'll be out there with the police, on the thin blue line between order and anarchy:

'Don't worry, Simon – we've got the scum nailed,' whispers Bryn in my ear. 'Oh yes! Today's going to be all downhill for someone.'

For our young managers, it really couldn't be a better start to the week. This is what adolescent males are all about: adrenaline overload in pursuit of narrow goals. They particularly love it when the fingerprints people turn up. SOCO, all right? Scene of Crime Officers, to the uninitiated.

'It's the dabs men,' says Bryn, for once oblivious to the woman on the team. He really must be excited.

We watch as SOCO unpack their gear – though it may have been their lunch, because some of it did go in the fridge.

'No questions today, Simon,' says Pinocchio, the boy-manager.

'I haven't asked any.'

'It's "schtumm" time.' Pinocchio taps his nose secretively, indicating that I should go back to the shop floor and continue with the girls' work, while he pursues James Bond operations backstage. And so we do. Unbothered by management, we start the early morning shelf fill, and consider their merits as detectives.

'Defectives, more like.'

'The Police Farce,' says Garry.

'So what exactly has happened?' asks Caspar.

Faith knows, because she has wheedled the information out of Bryn. It didn't take long. 'Whoever counted the money last night apparently took two thousand pounds for themselves. They came back after the shop closed.'

The thieves are applauded for their endeavour, but not for their brains, because there is a camera in the cash office. They were clearly the children in school who got full marks for effort – but not for getting the answers right.

As the morning progresses, the shop runs itself, as management stay backstage, hanging out with the police. They quickly learn the jargon and start talking to us about 'ongoing enquiries' and being 'unable to divulge information at this present moment pertinent to the investigation'. They also really like the police gadgets, discovering their radios to be much flasher than the breeze-block models we use in-store.

'Slightly embarrassing,' says Bryn, who is genuinely thinking about a change in career. 'What do you think, Si? Could you see me doing this?'

'I could see you messing up in a wide variety of settings.'

'Very funny – but I'm being serious.'

'And I'm not?'

Pinocchio is also in his element. He's never been so close to real police as this – yet now he's almost a policeman himself, giving vital information about security procedures. Heady stuff! You feel that if he was offered body armour for the day, he would take it. Meanwhile, it's hush-hush planning, in preparation for the 'hit' this afternoon. The staff are told nothing, apart from what Faith gets out of Bryn – which is everything. Approaching the toilet, I hear Pinocchio talking of a 'military operation'. The zero hour is clearly upon us.

The two members of staff come to work as usual, unaware of five policemen hidden behind the prawns. Pinocchio asks them into the office for a chat. Well, why not? Just a normal 'how are things going?' conversation with the staff – though in our store, that would be as normal as the Pope doing bakery. Anyway, the two seem happy enough to step inside – at which point the police swoop. And apart from tripping on a tray of strawberry yoghurt, it is a successful snatch.

The 'Cash Office Two' are questioned, handcuffed and removed for further questioning down at the nick. The customers love it, and should really have been charged extra, because get this – the two thieves are led out through the store itself. What entertainment! It's like the village stocks all over again – a ritual of comeuppance and humiliation. As one customer says: 'We should be allowed to give them a good kicking.'

The journey through the store was hardly necessary; there were more discreet exits. But what a 'Special Offer' for those waiting in the queue! For once, they are hoping not to be served, ushering others ahead of them: 'No, please – you first, I insist.'

'No, on the contrary, I insist – you must go before me! It's only a queue after all!'

Everyone is happy where they are, for here is a queue with a view. And because they are all looking at the shame and the handcuffs, no one notices the yoghurt on the sergeant's trousers.

🛒 🛒 🛒

But the question is: would I now be joining them, handcuffed and shamed? This was my fear as I made my way to the managers' office. I had a strong hunch I had been rumbled.

A few weeks after the cash theft, I was working on the till when Stav told me I must come to the office immediately: 'Finish serving the customer, and come to the office.'

'It's not a good time. We're busy.'

'Just do it.'

This was unusual. Management were usually directing me towards the till, not calling me away from it. Something was up, and I thought I knew what it might be. Not a morning went by, when putting out the produce, that I didn't enjoy the odd grape – or if the box broke, a few blueberries. Mohammed went a little further. I saw any broken carton as fair game, but if he was in a mood with the management, he saw any carton as fair game, broken or not. If it wasn't broken, it soon would be. It gave him pleasure to bring me the spoils, which I would be expected to share – and often did. So had I been found out?

I approached the office, entered, and saw Stav sitting at the desk. As you know, he is one of the four deputy managers, who serve under Pinocchio.

'Shut the door,' he says.

This is serious. The door is hardly ever closed. So what was it? The grapes, the blueberries or the mango pieces? If I have to go down for anything, I hope it's the latter, because they were very nice.

'Si,' says Stav, 'I need your help.'

'What sort of help?'

'You do writing sometimes, don't you?'

'I have in my past.'

'I need help with a letter. I'm applying for another job.'

'Oh.'

'With another company.'

'Really? I didn't know.'

'No one knows – and I don't want anyone to know. So this is secret, all right?'

'Fine. I'm Mr Secrets, I am.'

'But this is what I've done so far.'

He hands me a rough copy. 'Could you just take a look, and tell me what you think?'

We duly work on his secret job application, while the queues lengthen, and the lunchtime sandwiches fly off the shelves.

Suddenly Sapphy is in my ear.

'I gaw no money, Si!' she moans.

'You've got no money?'

'Gawer tii-en me bell this wee'!'

'Tighten your belt and you'll disappear, Sapphy.'

Despite her large consumption of food and alcohol, she looks like a winter sparrow. But money does come and go with her; there's nothing steady about Sapphy. She has either got no money at all for the next two weeks; or she's blowing huge sums on sunbeds, wild clubbing, and anything pink – after which she gets a taxi home. And of course supermarkets love people like this: people who see themselves both as saving the pennies and deserving the treats. Restraint and greed, restraint and greed – you can do both together here! You can both tighten your belt, and let it out, all at the same time. A miracle!

First, the restraint. To help you with this painful necessity, supermarkets offer endless savings and 'specials'. 'Three for two.' 'Buy one, get one free!' 'Six for five!' 'Twenty-seven for eighteen!' (I made that one up.)

But the fact is, every little helps.

So pay less – get more!

Us supermarkets – we're fools to ourselves!

And if supermarkets can't be bothered to lower the price, they just stick a shiny 'price watch' sticker on the product. It means nothing – but perpetuates delusions of thrift in the shopper.

'So what exactly does "Price watch" mean,' I ask Bryn, as we work together on the cheeses. Rotating the sell-by dates on the cheeses is a fiddly business, and no one likes this job.

'It means we've watched the price,' says Bryn.

'Right. But to what end?'

'How d'you mean?'

'Well, who actually gains from you watching the price?'

'I'm not personally watching the price, mate.'

'No, I know you're not, Bryn. You're watching the ladies.' Even as I speak, his eyes are wandering down the desserts aisle.

'She's nice,' he says.

'She's mine,' says Caspar, as he walks past.

'And the Price Watch?' I ask.

'Sorry?' says Bryn, who has lost track.

'You were telling me what "Price Watch" means.'

'The Price Watch? Well, it's to do with comparisons, isn't it, Si? Comparing like with like; across the board; the big picture.'

'Right.'

He seems happy with that answer, but I'm not. 'And when you've, er, compared like with like and all that – so what?'

Bryn pauses for a moment.

'Fuck knows,' he says, which is not supermarket orthodoxy, but often the correct answer.

But that's quite enough about restraint. Now for the good bit! After so much thrift and so much holding back, you wouldn't be human if you didn't desire a little treat or two; and supermarkets certainly want you to be human. You deserve it – you really do; especially in hard times like these. Go on, spoil yourself! So in the basket go the treats. Loads of them! And Sapphy agrees with all that: 'Ev'one nee's a trea' or two! Vat's wor I sii!'

She is saying that everyone needs a treat or two. That's what she says.

And at the end of it all – who exactly is the criminal here? It's hard to say, sometimes. Perhaps – and look away now if you haven't read it – it is like Agatha Christie's *Murder on the Orient Express*, where it's everyone. We all have our rules – and then we all bend them. We are all entirely consistent – until we are not. Our morality is a straight line, straight as a die – but with a few justifiable kinks. The Cash Office Two put a kink around taking money from a rich company that pays low wages. I put a kink around the fruit, because it is good for me, and it would only be thrown away if I didn't eat it. Stav puts a kink around using company time for his own purposes, because he doesn't owe them anything, after all the recent trouble with his wages. And daily, Pinocchio puts a kink around treating any of the staff with respect, because the company is here for profit not social work – and he doesn't know how to be anything other than negative. And supermarkets? Supermarkets put a kink around preying on vulnerable customers, because it's a free market, it's their choice, they're adults, and although the milk is put at the furthest point from the door, to ensure maximum exposure of all products – it's not as if customers *have* to buy anything. And the farmers can take what they're offered – or starve.

And Lenny? Lenny's kink was pastry. Lenny put a kink around a pain au chocolat from the bakery section, because he really fancied it – and was sacked last week for his troubles. He was out the door by lunchtime, though I think they wanted to get rid of him anyway, because truly, he was as lazy as a sloth in a hammock.

12.

WITCHES, WHIPS AND WICCA

In which we discover more about our in-store witch, Brian. We hear of his embarrassing conference incident; discover his remarkable IQ; visit his unusual home and discover 'The Magic Eight'.

Today, I am working with Brian, who is our resident witch.

'He's a witch,' said Stav, with a mischievous grin, on Brian's first day with us.

'How do you know?'

'He told me in the interview. Under hobbies. He's not ashamed or anything.'

'Fine,' I say, with some heaviness of heart. I didn't have a good image of witches. I could think only of *Macbeth*, and sad middle-aged men doing odd things in woods with goats' heads, fire and virgins.

'But a white witch,' said Stav. 'He said he was a white witch.'

'And the difference is?'

'I don't think they drink newt's blood.'

I confess to some assumptions when first Brian arrived in

the store. I know the saying: 'to assume is to make an ass of u and me' – but I still went ahead and did it, and wasn't best pleased when told he was working with me. After all, this was a supermarket – not a Harry Potter story.

'Seen the new sign in the cleaning cupboard, Si?' asks Caspar.

'No.'

'Brooms can only be used for cleaning.'

We are working together now. Brian and I have been putting out fruit and veg for about an hour, in silence. I have learned over the past few weeks, since his arrival, that he struggles with spontaneous questions; they can send him into a panic. Sometimes, though, if you wait long enough, he will spring into conversational life, and reveal all. He has, for instance, just been away on a witches' weekend conference, and apparently not all went to plan.

'I had a rather embarrassing encounter this weekend,' he says, out of the blue.

'Who with?'

'My ex-girlfriend.'

Ahh yes! He'd told me of her devastation when they split up a few months back. She had made the mistake of saying she loved him, and that, for Brian, was that. But just when he thought it was safe to go out, he happens to meet her again at a witches' conference. Life!

'So how did you meet?'

'It was after one of the sessions. I was up at the front, and she saw me.'

'Up at the front? That sounds important. What were you doing?'

'I was acting as the lay High Priest,' he says matter-of-factly.

Brian goes silent again. Have I asked too many questions?

'So what does a lay High Priest do?' I ask.

'He invokes the male deity.'

'Is there a female deity?'

'Yep. The lay High Priestess leads the invocation to her, obviously.'

Obviously. How could it be any other way?

He then tells me that there were meant to be belly dancers at the session, but they didn't turn up because one of them was pregnant. They did have some Morris dancers, however, who were fine until they started hectoring people to join in. As Brian hates being hectored, and hates dancing, this was not a good combination.

'Don't be shy!' said the man in funny clothes, and with bells round his knees.

Well, he clearly wasn't. Brian had quickly made his escape from the hall, before any damage was done. He stepped out into the sunlight with some relief. Phew! But it was on leaving the hall that he met his former girlfriend.

'Out of the frying pan, into the fire,' says Brian, drily.

🛒 🛒 🛒

On another occasion, and after much more silence, Brian suddenly tells me his IQ. This is not a subject I know anything about, but his score does sound a high one, and I make appreciative noises. You can't be a priest for twenty years without being able to spot when someone requires an affirmative grunt. That night, however, in order to discover more about the genius who works alongside me, I research further. And what do I find? I find a list of estimated IQs from history, which proves very revealing.

John Stuart Mill comes out top with 190, so well done him.

If this was the school prize-giving, he'd be walking away with the big one. But it's not just about the winner – so let's also give a round of applause to others who did well. Goethe came a very creditable second, clocking up 185, closely followed by the industrious Voltaire. Meanwhile, let's also hear it for Mozart and Byron on 150, Dickens on 145, and Wagner, Darwin, Beethoven and Leonardo da Vinci on 135.

I stop there, because just four below those beacons of excellence is Brian with 131. Wow! As a shop, we should be very proud he's with us; with perhaps a plaque by the potatoes, saying that Brian worked here. He may be quite the slowest stacker of shelves, and the most confused and chaotic of workers. But really – would Mill and Goethe have been any better with the parsnips? Would Byron and Voltaire have dazzled with the mushrooms? Darwin may have known all the species – but could he have stacked them? I doubt it.

And even as I recognise Brian for the intellectual demi-god he is, I am also remembering his performance at the Christmas party, when he really let himself go. He sang 'The Time Warp' in the karaoke session, and no one will forget it. They may wish to, but they will find themselves quite unable.

'Ee reelly came aa or 'imself wiv vat one,' said Sapphy.

And she was right. He never came out of himself enough to ask me a single question in two years of working with him – but he came out of himself that night; indeed he spilled all over the place, gyrating and screaming with some abandon. And with those images in mind, that may be the cue for visiting Brian at home. It's a little different.

Brian's landlady is a witch called Laura; and she's also a dom-inatrix. These are women who are paid to abuse, hurt and humiliate their clients, and in their professional life tend to be called things like 'Miss Whiplash', 'The Sex Matron' or 'Cruel Carla'.

'I have a room in the house,' says Brian. 'We share the kitchen.'

'And a front room?'

'There's no front room.'

'Every house has a front room.'

Pause.

'It's called "The Dungeon". No-go area.'

'Right.'

Humiliation is a profitable if competitive business, and Laura is trying to diversify into American Tribal Dancing. She runs a weekly class in a nearby community centre. It's women only, because she sees enough of men elsewhere. But it's early days for the venture, and her bread and butter remains the chain and the cane.

'Of course, Laura is also a trained nurse,' continues Brian matter-of-factly. 'Which is important.'

'Why?'

'Well – if you're inflicting pain on people, you have to be ready if something goes wrong.'

'I suppose.'

'And if the client is gagged, they can't explain their symptoms.'

This is true. It's difficult enough explaining symptoms to my doctor without a gag – but with one? And whilst on all fours?

Frequently Brian is woken at night by screams, because clients cannot always do office hours. Laura's husband Jim is also woken, and sometimes he and Brian meet in their pyjamas on the landing. Jim is an IT specialist, and never complains about his wife's shift work.

'But you do wonder what he's thinking,' says Brian. 'After all, it's his wife doing that downstairs.'

'I know what he's thinking,' says Caspar. ' "I wish she'd come and hit me once in a while!" '

And then, of course, there's Rex. Rex is another lodger in the house, who pays Laura to treat him badly on a permanent basis. He has to crawl everywhere, wears latex, and drinks his tea, and eats all his meals, from a dog bowl in the kitchen.

'The other night was particularly bad,' says Brian. 'Laura threw him out. I don't know what happened but Laura was very angry, and threw him out at midnight. He was back by the morning though.'

I was thinking it must be hard to punish those who seek punishment: 'Behave like that, and I'll treat you like a dog!'

'Thank you!'

Perhaps the only punishment for Rex is to treat him with extraordinary respect and kindness. 'Right! You've gone too far this time! There's no way back from here. We're through! From now on, I am going to honour you, and affirm your value and worth on this planet!'

'Oh no, please no – not that!'

Would that be the cruellest cut of all?

Perhaps one day, things will be different for them all. Perhaps one day, Brian will walk into the kitchen and be greeted not by a man on all fours, but by sunlight and an adoring wife; perhaps for Laura, tribal dancing is the beginning of a brand-new adventure; perhaps one day, Jim will get his nights back – oh, and the front room as well, replacing chains with chairs. And who knows? Perhaps Rex will get up off his knees, and finally remember who he is.

All things are possible.

Meanwhile, back in the store, other employees have their own misconceptions of witches. They find it hard to get past the childhood image of pointy hats, bubbling vats and black cats at midnight. This is hardly surprising. It's hard for anyone to get past their childhood images. Having been deeply absorbed by our soft skin and receptive minds, we adopt them unquestioningly as self-evident truth.

Occasionally, however, Brian takes me beyond the pointy hats, to the religion of Wicca, which is Brian's brand of paganism. 'It's a nature-based religion, originating in pre-Christian Europe,' he says, over the coleslaw. (We're putting it out – not eating it.)

Some say Wicca's origins are rather more recent, dating back only to the 1920s, but I don't mention this. He gets very defensive, very quickly.

'Nature-based? What does that mean?'

'Earth, air, fire, water and spirit are the five points of the pentagram, which is our symbol. Like Christians have the cross, we have the pentagram.'

Brian seems pleased with the lesson so far, but then goes silent, and we do not return to the subject for another couple of weeks, when he talks of the law of threefold return.

'The Law of Threefold return means what it says,' states Brian. 'Whatever benevolent or malevolent action a person performs, will return to that person with triple force.'

'It's a bit like the eastern idea of karma, I suppose.'

Brian doesn't answer, so I continue: 'Or there's another saying, which is similar: "Your being attracts life". In other words, what you are inside, you inevitably draw towards you. Unhappy people draw unhappiness towards themselves;

happy people draw happiness.'

Again, Brian doesn't answer. I must allow for the fact that this conversation is on his terms. He doesn't discuss – he lectures. Questions threaten him, but he will tell me things if I wait long enough. And in time, he reveals that followers of Wicca worship a God and a Goddess, sometimes symbolised as the sun and the moon; that some feminist Wicca believe there's only a Goddess; that yes, they do cast spells through the form of ritual practices; and that they believe in reincarnation.

He then takes me into new territory, listing the eight Wicca virtues. 'Mirth, reverence, honour, humility, strength, beauty.'

'Well, you can't knock any of those!' I say, and then wait for the rest, conscious that was only six. But Brian stops there, seemingly satisfied.

'That's six,' I say.

'Er, yes.'

There is an awkward moment, in which he feels exposed. I think he was hoping I hadn't noticed, and now he's struggling with the idea that he may have forgotten two of Wicca's eight virtues. (We must hope that one of them doesn't turn out to be 'A good memory'.)

'Well, that's a pretty good six,' I say, trying to lessen the pain. 'And who knows all the Ten Commandments anyway? Not many in my experience. I could never quite get all ten in one go. I'd always leave out coveting, or adultery or false witness – or most often, the graven images.'

'Power,' says Brian, firmly.

'Power?'

'Power. That's one of the eight virtues.'

'Ah.'

I'm less impressed by that one; power is too ambiguous to

be a virtue in itself. But I'm glad he's got there; or nearly got there. We are now one virtue away from Valhalla. Brian is looking intently at the spring onions, and I am rotating the cucumbers when finally enlightenment strikes:

'Compassion,' he says, 'that's the other one.'

And with that, he strides off down the aisle towards the bananas. He clearly needs to be away from me. The exertions of conversation have left him shell-shocked and unsettled. He needs to be alone with fruit which doesn't pester him with questions.

He did return to the theme later when he said, by way of nothing at all, 'The 2001 census – forty-two thousand declared themselves to be "pagans".'

People do laugh about Brian behind his back; and certainly the 'witch' label doesn't help. But in the end, we are known for who we are; not the label we stick on ourselves. Of the eight Wicca virtues, perhaps 'honour' is his strong hand. Home sweet home is not all it might be for Brian; but he is an honourable man amid the fruit and veg.

13.

MY TREVOR'S LIKE
SATAN – HELP!

*In which the man with no name meets
his match and Winston reveals his
laundry secrets. Sapphy is told of
impending motherhood; Dave the
smooth family doctor advises desperate
Maxine; little Mal stacks fruit; little
Jane spells it – and Omar gets the
message. Oh yes!*

A supermarket initiative is something that takes six months to plan, one month to communicate and about two days to forget. They are created by people who need to be planning to give their lives meaning. But this does not mean that what they create has meaning.

Initiatives come and go in supermarkets, like the minutes of the day. Tick-tock, tick-tock and another initiative is launched, promoted, explained and forgotten. Tick-tock, tick-tock go the minutes of our lives, as new procedures arrive from on high. Tick-tock, tick-tock as a fresh paper-fall of leaflets appears on the table – pushy, pressing and here to make things better; raise standards and improve our poor performance. Ahoy there! Fresh initiative approaching! Nothing is ever going to be the same again — honestly!

'Listen up, guys,' says Bryn, at this morning's team briefing. 'Has everyone read the "Name Badge" leaflet?'

No one has, which is a shame, because name badges are today's 'very important new initiative'.

'Does everyone remember the visit of the Mystery Shopper last week?' asks Bryn.

Cue the opening bars of Beethoven's fifth symphony — de, de, de daaah! — in order to establish scary atmosphere. It may be only 7.00 am, but suddenly everyone's awake. Mystery Shoppers? Yikes! Mystery Shoppers are paid to visit the store incognito, as normal customers, and assess the place. A week after their visit, the store duly receives its rating. And we have just received ours — a rating considerably damaged by the fact that two of us were not wearing our name badges. Bryn is going ballistic, in a chummy look-guys-I-just-have-to-do-this! sort of a way.

'Seriously — you have to have a name badge. And two of you didn't last Thursday.'

'Who?' asks Caspar.

'They shall remain nameless,' says Bryn.

Everyone collapses in laughter.

'Look, all right, we don't know who they were,' says Bryn, trying to save face.

'Incognito,' says Caspar. 'Wise move. That way, no one can touch you.'

'You shouldn't be on the shop floor without a name badge. That's the bottom line.'

'I'm still waiting for mine,' says Caspar.

'Every member of staff has two,' says Bryn.

'Two don't last very long. They come off.'

'And they fuck up the washing machine,' adds Garry.

'Then take them off beforehand,' says Bryn.

'Tell my mum,' says Garry.

'I cannot believe your mum still does your washing,' says Winston.

'I'm only forty-eight,' he replies. 'And she likes doing it.'

'My mother last did my washing when I was fourteen years old,' says Winston.

'Not surprised. She probably doesn't like you,' says Faith rather cruelly. It's cruel because it's probably true. 'I wouldn't do your washing either.'

'Neither would I ever consider asking you,' replies Winston, haughtily.

'And I wouldn't if you did.'

'And equally, I wouldn't give you my clothes even if you begged me,' said Winston, straying into the territory of highly unlikely events.

'Me ask for your dirty clothes?!' Faith sucks her teeth in disdain. 'Like that's going to happen.'

'All interesting stuff, but we're drifting,' says Bryn. 'You're all Clint Eastwood out there – the man with no name – and head office is going mental. So today, everyone is to have a name badge.'

'My mum stopped washing my clothes,' continues Winston, 'for one reason, and one reason only – because at the age of fourteen, I said I was well capable of doing it myself. End of story.'

Bryn then brings round a plastic container full of the name badges of past workers in the store; badges no longer needed by their wearers, for they have passed through to the other side; moved on to higher things.

'Until the new ones come in,' says Bryn, 'those who need a badge will wear one from this box.'

Sadly, boys are not allowed to choose girls' names and vice versa. So in the end, I choose 'Omar' and remain Omar for the next few months. I am surprised how quickly I get used to my new identity, making me aware of how meaningless names are. Like store initiatives, they come and go.

🛒 🛒 🛒

Jesus was unusual in encouraging the presence of children. 'Let the children come to me,' he famously said – 'for they are the Kingdom of God in our midst.'

Supermarkets, however, have mixed feelings about them: let the children come to me, as long as they're not being stupid in the aisles or throwing a wobbly in the queue. Sapphy, for instance, loves babies who chuckle and smile and Cheeky Chappy toddlers.

'U gor a nor-ee li'al smile, u hav!'

She doesn't, however, like moany children, or children who cry all the time. They really get on her nerves.

'Why doan vey juzz shu-arp!' she says despairingly, as a yelling child finds no peace; and gives none to anyone else.

A conversation starts on the tills about children.

'I mea' doan get me wrong,' says Sapphy. 'I luv kids, an' of course I'd lii to 'av some of me own. Juzz doan know if I could pu'arp wiv vem.'

'And the other consideration is whether they could put up with you,' says Winston.

'Children are a pain,' says Faith.

Faith likes her children for entertainment, and the funny things they say, but is not so good when they reach up for a cuddle. Her eldest boy is currently in three sorts of trouble with the police.

'Best to have a lot of them,' she says, 'and then they can look after themselves.'

She pauses, and then adds with a glint in her eye: 'You know Ola wants children, Sapphy; many many children!'

'Why you lookin' at me?' asks Sapphy.

'He said you are to be married.'

'Eee nevaar! Me an' Ola?!'

But she can't help but blush.

Customers don't generally bring children to the supermarket out of choice. Supermarkets are a favourite place for tantrums and mad writhing on the floor, in determined and noisy despair. And the children are just as bad. Doctors and psychologists can earn a little holiday money by writing Saturday columns or doing radio slots advising parents on how to handle children in supermarkets:

> Dear Dave, the smooth family doctor,
> I love my little Trevor to bits, but in a supermarket he becomes like Satan! Please help. Is there anything I can do?
> Desperate by the desserts,
> Maxine,
> Middlesbrough.

> Dear Maxine,
> Being a parent myself, I know how you feel! And certainly I have no magic wand to wave. But how about bringing Trevor into the whole shopping process? Perhaps he could help you draw up the shopping list, for instance. What does he want? What do you want? Work together on it. And then once there, how about

> letting him help to find the items? Give him some
> responsibility, and you might just find there's a change in him –
> less satanic, hopefully! Good luck!
> Dave, the smooth family doctor.

I came across a hand-out once. On one side, there were seven
signs of the 'good enough' parent; on the other, seven signs
of the 'not-so-good' parent. I adapted it a bit, and kept it. First,
a description of the 'good enough' parent:

1) Strong enough to carry several dependent people for two
   decades.
2) Mindful of the needs of those who have not yet
   developed the capacity to express themselves.
3) With a lively interest in people and social activities.
4) With an interest in their own life-adventure. When
   approaching death, they wish to look back on a life
   grasped and lived.
5) Is encouraging to be with, and encourages a sense of
   adventure in those around them.
6) Lives neither in the past nor in the future – but in the
   present.
7) Aware that in both good times and bad times, this too
   shall pass.

And then the 'not-so-good':

1) Uses the child to satisfy their own needs for fun, compan-
   ionship, power or control.
2) Uses emotional or physical power to frighten or manipulate children.
3) Will always think they know best; unable to imagine that
   anyone else's values could be worthwhile.
4) A negative presence, emphasising what could go wrong,

or how something could be done better.

5) Too full of unresolved anger or grief to give time to another soul.

6) Feels like a doormat, at everyone's beck and call – tired, irritated, resentful or burnt out.

7) Inconsistent in their dealings with their children, everything being dependent on their mood.

I'm all fourteen, of course – but I'd prefer to be just seven.

🛒 🛒 🛒

When I think of the children in the supermarket, I think of a four-year-old called Mal who always comes to help me. His single mum leaves him with me while she gets on with the shopping – and on one occasion, actually nips out to get a coffee from Starbucks down the road. Mal is limited in what he can do when it comes to shelf filling. He's not strong enough to lift the trays from the stack, and neither is he tall enough to reach even the lowest shelf in the chiller cabinet. He can't read any of the labels either. But set against these constraints is his brightness of spirit, and a get-up-and-go attitude, which my colleague Brian could learn from.

Or I think of little Jane, who comes with her bleak father.

'Those are pineapples,' he says. 'What are they, Jane?'

'Pineapples,' says Jane dutifully.

'And those are mangoes,' says her father. 'What are they?'

'Mangoes.'

'Spell "mango".'

'M-a-n-g-o.'

'Quite an easy one that. These are pears. What are they?'

'Pears.'

'And these?'

'Er — I don't know.'

'They're apricots. You should know that by now! Apricots. Spell apricots.'

Jane will become herself again — perhaps many years hence — when she can look on fruit not as a test, or spelling list to be learned, but as something colourful, tasty, aromatic and completely wonderful.

My final experience of a parent today, however, shortly before I leave, is a mum who uses her children as a conduit to express her anger with the store. Through exaggerated speech, she talks through the child, to me, standing close by.

'What a cold, cold shop, Claudia! Such a cold shop! Whatever happened to the heating?' she says. And then turning towards her son: 'And no organic raspberries, Peter. None yesterday, none today! Now that's not very good, is it? Not very good at all!'

Claudia is as warm as toast, and Peter is three, and doesn't know what a raspberry is — but this is not the point. This isn't kids' stuff. The message is for Omar.

14.

EVE'S DOWNFALL AND REALLY RUBBISH CUSTOMERS

In which we meet shoppers various;
have issues with the apples; encounter
Simon's least favourite customer; hear
the intriguing results of the hospital
test, and insult Edna and Margaret.

Everyone has their own approach to supermarkets. Not everyone likes them, of course, but everyone must relate somehow. Looking around me as the day unfolds, I see all the types. There are some who rush in to grab a specific and urgent item − perhaps a croissant or a sandwich − and that's it. In, out, job done − and these are called the *Briefs*. Others meander dreamily through, with a child in tow, a Costa coffee to their lips, and a whole morning to fill. Time is not pressing in any way at all, and decisions can take hours − and these are the *Wanderers*. Some know what they want, want what they know, complain at will, and destroy every display to find the best sell-by date. These are the *Pushies*. Others arrive in military fashion, with long lists, deep trolleys, no time, no manners and large cars, to claim their ample provisions for the next month. God help anyone who slows or threatens their advance. These are the *Bastards*. And of course some don't come in at all, but distribute leaflets outside – and these are called the *Friends of the Earth*.

This morning, however, you discover me stacking apples, and I have to say, beautiful though they are – apples can be irritating. I like to eat them, but not to stack them, and here's why. As you know, all food must be rotated, with the later sell-by date at the back. It's the number one rule in the supermarket. Rotation, rotation, rotation. Clever-dick customers know this, of course, and reach for the back so instinctively that I sometimes wonder whether if it wouldn't be wiser to put the new stuff at the front – and then watch the smart-aleck shoppers taking home the really old yoghurt.

'Result!'

Alternatively, when Miss Best-Possible-Sell-By-Date-For-Me-Always! approaches, place a rat trap at the back of the shelf.

'Snap!'

The customer may always be right, but that doesn't mean their cockiness should go unpunished.

Now you may think such thoughts unworthy, and indeed they are – but it's probably better to tell it as it is, rather than how we'd like it to be. Everyone knows how we'd like to be: kind, discerning, just, fulfilled, passionate, content, generous, courageous and open. But in the meantime, while waiting for enlightenment, we waste our lives imagining stupid stunts with old yoghurts and rat traps at the back of shelves.

But getting back to the apples – 'because they don't stack themselves!' as one customer helpfully tells me – I have a problem. Like everything else, apples should be rotated – but 'Eve's Downfall' makes it hard, since they are not in a row, but a pile. So what do you do? Theoretically, you should remove all existing stock from the holders, put all the new stock in at the bottom, and then put the old stuff on top. But would you? Really?! Or might you think, 'Frankly, I can't be bothered this morning', and shove the new stuff on top? Perhaps it would at least cross your mind. It does cross mine.

Apart from anything else, there are just so many different sorts of apple to display. Red Delicious, Granny Smiths, Braeburns, Cox's, Jazz, Royal Galas, Tentations and Pink Ladies have all travelled miles by plane to be with us today. Fortunately, they're so drugged up with preservatives that they are in no particular hurry. After all, some were picked over a year ago, and have sat patiently in chiller cabinets around the world, waiting their turn. A day or so more will hardly hurt.

There's one of those healthy posters above my head which declares: 'There's nothing like fresh fruit!'

And truly, this is nothing like fresh fruit. For fresh fruit, best to get down to the local Farmers' Market. And it is just as I think these disloyal thoughts that I see my worst customer approaching.

I do not bestow 'worst customer' accolade lightly – for I'm not short of candidates. Daily, shoppers are rude or abrasive, treating us as beings with neither intelligence nor feelings. But they are not the worst customers. Also on the short list is the man who recently hit me, when I challenged him about thieving. Pinocchio, our boy-manager, came over. But far from supporting me, he just nodded intently at the thief – as if this disturbed and disjointed soul was the author of The Seven Pillars of Wisdom.

Here was a man who had hit me, missed with some spit,

and generally raged in my face. Yet, dear reader, this was not my least favourite customer. For worse than being treated as nothing, and worse than being spat at and hit, is being patronised – aka being treated like scum politely. And it is about to happen again as my worst customer approaches. She has seen me, and more worryingly, has seen that I have seen her. So there is no way out; I must face the darkness.

'How are we today?' she asks.

We? I look round, expecting to see a crowd behind me. Surprisingly, I found myself alone.

'I'm sparkling, thanks.'

This is what I always say.

'Good, good,' she says, with condescension, while getting on with the more important business of choosing a salad. It's enough that she says words to me; she shouldn't have to engage with me as well. 'Jolly good for you,' she adds.

'And you?' I ask. 'How are things with you?'

'I'm glad it's all going so well for you,' she replies, ignoring my enquiry as she removes some couscous from the shelf. 'Jolly good.'

Did I not ask a question? Am I suddenly speaking in a foreign tongue? Do I exist? And of course the short answer is that I don't exist. Those who patronise others must stake everything on them not existing; or existing as only half-beings, who appear on earth solely to bolster their own fragile self-worth. But I have my own weapon, and decide to use it. I have no wish to collude in the illness of another.

'You're definitely looking a bit down,' I say.

Marvellous! It's like holding up a cross to a vampire. Suddenly she is presented with the idea that she is not completely in charge of this relationship; that in some way, it's a two-way affair; that in fact – whisper it quietly – I might even be the stronger one this morning!

'Down? Down?! I haven't time to be down, young man! Much too busy!'

And with that she scuttles away like an irritated crab, her exoskeleton hardening to cover the rage and confusion inside.

'Thank you for patronising our store, madam,' I say, as I return to the apples.

🛒 🛒 🛒

People do not intend to be rude, of course. They do not wake up in the morning and think, 'Today I will be unpleasant in a supermarket.' It's just that people panic when their fragile hold on life seems under threat. People need to believe they are in control of their lives, and when this is revealed not to be so, they become as frightened toddlers. Remember Banana Woman not finding what she wanted, and screaming: 'This shop is like the bloody third world!' – before storming out.

And neither do people intend to hate. They do not wake in the morning and think, 'Today I will hate someone in the supermarket.' It's just that people panic when their fragile hold on life seems under threat, and standing in a queue can be one of those times: 'Why aren't things moving faster?' they think. 'Why are the cashiers talking to the customers as they serve them? Just get on with it! These other people may have all the time in the world, but I haven't! And do they have to take quite so long to weigh the fruit? Oh, and what's gone wrong now – surely they don't need to call over a manager about that item? They do?! Can't they deal with anything themselves? It's hardly rocket science! And what now?! The till roll needs changing? Oh my God! I don't believe it! I mean, can't they all be changed at the beginning of the day? They're monkeys

– the lot of them! Who's in charge here? And how long does it take to sort out someone's change?!'

And so on and so forth.

It can be unnerving to look up from the till and see pure hate in someone's eyes, directed at you. They do not know you, but they hate you for revealing to them that they are not in control. No one thanks you for that.

And as I wander these bright aisles of mad and frenetic acquisition, I often think of a story told me a long time ago when I was training to be a priest. It was told as a true story, of a test done in a hospital, about good and bad influences on us. A group of students were told to walk down a long corridor, in order to get to another part of the hospital. Halfway down the corridor was a man in some distress. Before they left, half the students were told the story of the Good Samaritan. In this story told by Jesus, a man lies injured by the side of the road after being attacked. Two supposedly holy people then approach, but both walk past the man, who is ignored, until a Samaritan arrives, sees the need, and stops to help. The researchers were interested to know whether the students who heard this story were more likely to stop in the corridor and help the man in distress.

As it turned out, it made no difference at all. Some stopped to help, some didn't – but it was not contingent on having heard the story. What I most remember, however, was the other piece of information they gleaned in the experiment. Because apart from some being told the Samaritan story, there was another difference between the students – half of them were specifically told to hurry. And guess what? None of those ones stopped. Not one.

Hurry takes us out of the present, and makes monsters of us all. But, thankfully, Edna and Margaret are never in a hurry.

They are two sisters in their eighties and they visit the store about twice a week. One carries the basket, and the other decides what goes in and pays for it all at the tills.

'Didn't see you last time,' says Edna, catching me gazing out of the window. 'You been away – or just skiving?'

'You know I always try and avoid you,' I say. I'm always rude to those I'm fond of.

'You rude young man!' exclaims Margaret, in delighted offence. 'Where's the manager – I want to complain!'

'The manager? He wouldn't talk with you – you don't spend enough. You have to spend over twenty pounds to qualify for decent customer service here.'

'Ooh, the cheek!'

Margaret and Edna were in retail themselves, know the game, and as we compare managers of the 1950s with now, we discover that nothing much has changed. They had some shockers too.

'Mr Bryant was the best, though,' says Edna. 'A very firm man. You didn't take liberties with him – but when you needed help, eh, Margaret?'

'Oh yes. When you needed help, he was wonderful,' said Margaret. 'No, he was.'

And Edna and Margaret are wonderful too; my favourites, in fact.

15.

CRUMBS OF COMFORT

*In which Simon makes a decent crust
and Mohammed and Sapphy get fed.
Caspar and Rosemary clash; Robert
gets sacked; Mr and Mrs Bigot turn on
Faith, and the health and safety debate
continues on and on and on...*

Today I'm on bakery – so I'm making a good crust, even if I'm not earning one. I replace Faith when she has a day off, holidays, or is required to attend one of her son Jason's many court appearances. Today I am here because recently he was caught in a dark shop doorway carrying a large metal implement.

'He's a good boy, but easily misled,' says Faith, in familiar parental denial. As if Jason's issues are anything to do with her!

But here's the upside. I'm delighted to be doing bakery. On bakery I become someone special, with a distinctive uniform – apron and cool baseball hat. (You're meant to wear a hairnet as well, but let's be honest – I'm too bald to qualify.)

There are certain sacrifices on bakery, of course. First of all, you have to hit the ground running; get going straight away. While others wander aimlessly around with their hot chocolate, taking in the magazine section on their travels, you have to have the oven on, and be laying out the croissants.

By 8.30 am – as bleary-eyed commuters gather at the bus stop outside – much of your work is done.

Secondly, though much time is spent by the oven, there are also regular forays into the freezer, which is really very cold. There is a sort of wonder stepping into this sudden polar region of steaming cold. But if you don't wear the special coat and gloves, and fail to find the boxes you want immediately – then the pain is quite sudden, and the wonder quickly lost.

And finally, of course, on the theme of self-sacrifice, it is best for everyone's sake, when baking, not to pick your nose – particularly when someone is watching. It can do long-lasting damage to sales.

But the pay-off for such self-discipline is huge. You are given not only a uniform but a kingdom of your own in which to create something that both looks wonderful and smells wonderful. Earth has nothing to show more fair than my display of croissants, Danish pastries, pains au chocolat and almond loaf. Wow!

'Look and wonder,' I say to Caspar, who is on one of his walk-abouts, strutting past the checkout girls like a peacock.

'Not bad,' he says.

'Not bad? Not bad?! It's brilliant!'

'You've been learning from the master.'

'That's right – self-taught.'

'Look, Si – you know I wrote the book when it comes to bakery display,' he says. 'But at least you've read it and learned.'

This is true, in a way. Caspar is excellent at display; and really he should be doing bakery this morning, because he is better at it than me. But he doesn't like getting tied down to the ovens – it would cramp the wanderer's style. How could he go walkabout if tied to the clock-watching and constant activity of the bakery game? And how could he wind up Rosemary –

because yes, he was the cause of a terrible row in the warehouse earlier.

As you know, Caspar calls Rosemary 'the Poison Dwarf' because she's short and poisonous. She has recently complained that the trays of meat are stacked too high for her to work from. So this morning, the warehouse team, guided by Caspar, responded. Instead of wheeling out the usual stack of eight trays on the trolley, they brought just one. Tiny Rosemary towered over it like Gulliver in Lilliput.

'Hope it's not too high, Rosemary,' said Caspar. 'If it is, tell us – and we'll just bring out the trolley next time.'

'You are so childish,' sneered Rosemary.

'It's a pleasure.'

Rosemary stormed off to the managers' office to complain – but with little effect. Once they're all settled in with their coffees and boys' chat about mortgages and fast cars, it's quite hard to disturb them.

'Sort it out yourself, Rosemary, for God's sake!'

Un-dealt with, the rage doesn't go away – just sinks below the waterline. Cold wars are dangerous, however, with a tendency suddenly to heat up. And when Robby from the warehouse swore at Rosemary a few weeks later, she made her move, and this time, caught the tide. She complained to the managers and found ready ears. Instead of waving her away as a tiresome nutcase, they noted everything she said. Robby's timekeeping had been poor, and this was just what they needed to sack him. He was gone by the end of the day. Rosemary's stock sank even lower in the shop, as a result; but maybe she thought it was worth it.

They do say that vengeance is a dish best served cold; though my feeling is that it's best not served at all.

I have had to sack people in my time. I remember one caretaker I employed. He had not only stopped caretaking a while back – but was now becoming aggressive towards various members of staff, and destructive in meetings. He was ex-Army, a violent man, and I was not looking forward to explaining the bad news. At best, I expected damage to property; at worst, damage to me – and I remember asking a number of people to pray for me as the day approached.

On Monday morning, after a brief team meeting, I asked to speak with him. We went and sat in my office. It wasn't the time for polite conversation.

'Danny – I think it might be time for you to go.'

How would he react? From which angle would the assault come?

'OK,' he said – and from that day on until he left three weeks later, he was as docile as a lamb. It was almost as if it was a personal relief for him; that he could now get on with being human again.

And me? I could laugh at my fears.

This morning, however, many years on, and with two good hours of baking behind me, I am looking with pride on my work. I think again of Wordsworth as he gazed on early morning London: 'Dull would he be of soul, who could pass by a site so touching in its majesty.'

But maybe Pinocchio, our boy-manager, is dull of soul, for he passes by my display a few times and finds it neither touching nor majestic. As always, he slides around the store on the soles of his shoes, to let you know he's around – and that you're probably not doing a very good job. There's always a negative tilt in the dull of soul; and, sadly, I have never heard him compliment anyone on anything in the store. On this occasion, he simply says: 'Don't put too much out, Simon. We've had to throw away some recently.'

A little later, I notice Mohammed hanging around bakery, like a seagull over a trawler.

'Anything?' he asks.

I know what he's getting at. Just as I believe in common land, I believe also in common bakery – always ensuring there's a suitable number of 'broken bits' to pass on to staff. I take him behind the display, away from nosy and incriminating cameras.

'There are some chocolate chip cookies,' I say.

Mohammed consumes them quickly, and is visibly refreshed. 'Very good,' he says, and returns to the vegetables rubbing his stomach. He has enjoyed both eating the food – and the company profits.

And then Sapphy turns up: 'Ee ain eee em orr?' she asks with feeling.

'No, he hasn't eaten them all,' I reassure her. 'There'll be more.'

'Well, I 'ope so!'

'I've put some damaged muffins in the canteen. They're in the bag on the side.'

'Fangs, Si!'

Why does no one eat breakfast these days?

As I say, Faith usually does bakery, and unlike me, looks very sexy in her apron. Men are understandably disappointed when it's me.

'Is she not here then?' asks Larry the Lecher. 'The girl – not in today?'

'Away on holiday,' I say, and even as I speak, his eyes are

drifting towards Sapphy.

Faith performs the baking role with a professionalism I can only dream of. Apart from anything else, she can gossip and keep a close eye on the baguettes at the same time. This is partly because she never gives conversation much of her attention; but also due to her ease with the baking. For me, it remains something of an amateur adventure – and perhaps the better for that.

But you are in the public eye on bakery, and the public eye can be pretty condemning. Faith recently had a bad bust-up with some customers over some apple turnovers. It happened like this: Faith used her bare hands to put out some apple turnovers. A couple saw this and started shouting.

'I don't want your black hands on my food!' said the man, in a manner which brought the whole shop to a standstill. Years of racial tension held within had suddenly exploded.

'That's disgusting!' shouted his wife.

'We saw what you did – and it's not acceptable in this country!'

'We'll have the shop closed down!'

'And you sent back home!'

Faith was just beginning to fight back when Pinocchio came sliding over. A deputy manager led the fuming Faith away, while Pinocchio eagerly licked the bigot's boots. In circumstances such as this, employees are always to be sold down the river by management, and Faith certainly was. Back in the warehouse, however, the racist implications of the episode were sinking in, and once they had, Faith was not slow to spread the news. I heard from every black member of staff within the hour.

'That behaviour should be challenged,' they say.

'By who?'

'By Pinocchio.'

'Pinocchio challenge a customer? You're having a laugh. The

sun will cool before that happens.'

I promise to take it up with him, however. We shall not go gently into that good night of bigotry. And we shall rage, rage against the dying light of respect.

🛒 🛒 🛒

Of course, hygiene is one of those areas where perception is everything. There's more nasty stuff on our food than we'd ever wish to know; yet what the eye doesn't see the heart doesn't grieve over. What the eye does see, however, causes great panic.

I remember a particularly awkward moment when as a priest I was in my most public of positions – standing at the altar, in front of an expectant congregation. Before me was a large silver goblet of wine. In the service, the wine is blessed before being passed around to each member of the congregation to drink. I looked out on their faces – and then down at the wine, and realised I had a problem. For floating in the wine were three dead flies. How they had got there, I didn't know, but it was too late to turn back now. Clearly, I couldn't pass the goblet around, with three flies a-floating. Everyone would see them. But then again, how was I to remove them?

Well, the basic rule for public action is this: 'Whatever you do – do it with confidence.' And so I did. Dressed in my priestly robes, and aware of the theatre of it all, I thrust my fingers down into the wine once, twice, three times. From a distance, it probably looked like a particular sort of Trinitarian blessing. But each time my fingers went in, they removed a fly – one, two, three – and then I carried on. It probably all looked very holy.

And back in supermarket world, the health and safety debate goes on. What should Faith have done with the apple turnovers

– apart from throw them at Mr and Mrs Bigot?

'We need to talk about bakery,' says Stav in the team briefing following the incident, by which time tempers have calmed a little.

The thing is, we do have plastic gloves for use in the bakery, but have been told not to use them – for health and safety reasons. Apparently, it's reckoned that the chemicals in the gloves react dangerously to contact with hot food. This shows either a slight lack of foresight by the manufacturers – or research. But really, which of us isn't guilty of that occasionally?

'So how are we supposed to pick them up?' I ask.

'Just use tongs,' says Stav.

'As opposed to tongues,' says Caspar.

'Or thongs,' says Garry, as serious health and safety debate comes to an end.

౼ ౼ ౼

As I say, I enjoy bakery: the initial burst of energy, and then the quiet tending of the plot as the day unfolds. Wisdom generally lies not in dramatic gesture, but quiet tending, so the bakery is a good teacher. It is the baguettes which most commonly need refilling; and sometimes the croissants. One customer, recently back from a holiday in France, even declared our croissants to be better than theirs. Zut alors!

And then, when waiting for the oven to do its work, and with nothing else to do, I think of whose steps I follow here. Hafiz, the wonderful Sufi poet of the fourteenth century – he was once a baker. Orphaned at an early age, he was employed by a baker, as a dough maker. When managers are mean or customers curt, this historical solidarity is an undoubted crumb of comfort.

16.

SORRY SEEMS TO BE THE HARDEST WORD

In which an apology appears out of the question. We deal with yoghurt-shaped disappointment; and enter the netherworld of Toad's induction course.

The world's religions and secular humanism may not agree about much – but they do agree about saying sorry. They may all hate each other most of the time – but all find something healthy in an apology. Such things as a bowed head, and a sense of regret and sadness – they can even get you a reduced sentence in court. An apology is a powerful and universal thing; and support for it, a small island of unity in the Sea of Separation. At last – something we all share! A truth we can all own and celebrate! Hallelujah! Perhaps the world can be saved? We all agree about something – we agree it's good to apologise!

Except for supermarkets, obviously.

Whatever we think of supermarkets, once they appear on a high street near us, they are quite hard to avoid – being well stocked with everything we like, and with sell-by dates we can trust. OK, so the local Budgetmart is nearer and always open, but there are issues: it smells of old socks, the boy behind the counter always tries it on with the change, and there's no question they alter the dates on the pitta bread. Complain, however, and you are suddenly surrounded by four members of the family, three of whom kill. You might as well have insulted their mother.

This is not like the supermarket. Oh no! Complain to the manager in the supermarket and he's all over you like a rash, offering the world in reparation. Budgetmarts take things personally, but supermarkets play the long game. They want to be fleecing you this time next year. Only don't expect an apology.

If you take your complaint high enough in a supermarket, you'll get reparation. They'll exchange your bag of slightly tart oranges, or refund you for the dented can of beans. These things are easily done, and quite painless; an exchange of product, or a little money from the till. But an apology? That's something else entirely. An apology suggests that the store has failed you, and of course the store never fails anyone.

'That isn't the message we want to give.'

'What is the message we want to give?'

'It's about being positive.'

'But what if we fail?'

'Re-frame it. Make it a success.'

'Re-frame it?'

'You have to realise that we are in a highly competitive market, Simon. People need to leave the store feeling they are part of a success story.'

And this explains why, on the shop floor, we are forbidden to use the word 'unfortunately'. We can't say it. I may use it six times a day when talking to customers, but this is blatant rule-breaking. As far as the company is concerned, 'unfortunately' is an evil word. It suggests we have let the customer down in some way, which is a real marketing gaffe. If the customer feels let down, they might take their business elsewhere; and that is the end of the world – an abyss too frightening even to contemplate.

So here's how to handle it – 'best practice' you might say, and I offer it free of charge: the customer desperately wants some rhubarb yoghurt, and there's none on the shelves. OK. You acknowledge the absence, and go off and look in the cold store.

'I'll be back in a moment, madam.'

You make your way to the cold store, but on arrival, discover that there is no rhubarb yoghurt there either. We clearly have none in the store – and there isn't another delivery until tomorrow. You now return to the customer – but be careful; be very careful. Whatever you do, don't say: 'I'm very sorry, madam, but unfortunately it's out of stock.'

Instead, establish the facts concerning the rhubarb yoghurt – that it is unavailable – and then politely but firmly re-direct the customer's attention to another product:

'We are currently experiencing a short-term non-availability scenario with regard to the rhubarb yoghurt, madam, but I wonder – have you considered our prawn balls?'

$$\text{🛒 🛒 🛒}$$

In failing to acknowledge how the customer feels, the store is displaying a worrying lack of emotional intelligence. Ride roughshod over feelings, and you are inviting trouble – no matter how wonderful or large your prawn balls. In this situation, each customer is to be compared to a hurting baby – and the first thing they need is their discomfort acknowledged.

'So you haven't got any rhubarb yoghurt?'

'Unfortunately not.'

'I was banking on that.'

'I'm very sorry. It's irritating, I know.'

'And you're sure there's none out the back?'

'Yes, I've checked. We had some yesterday, and we'll have some tomorrow – but that doesn't help you right now. As I say, I'm very sorry.'

'Trouble is – he only likes the rhubarb.'

'And that makes it difficult for you, doesn't it?'

'It does, yes.'

'I wish I could be more help.'

'Oh, it's not your fault. I suppose I could try him on the black cherry. Might be good for him to try something else.'

Disappointment is a daily occurrence. We'll be disappointed in some way or other three times before lunch; and in the end, we must deal with it ourselves, and heal our selves. But we are greatly helped in this adventure if our hurt is acknowledged by someone else. And the bigger the disappointment, the more important such acknowledgement is.

For many, losing someone they love is the worst disappointment of all. And I have sat with many of these.

'Nothing means anything to me now.'

'No.'

'To think we'll never go cycling again.'

'You went cycling together?'

'Went all over the place! Won't be doing that any more.'

The woman looks out of the window, as if remembering. And then continues. 'Would have been his birthday next Tuesday.'

'That will be very hard. Anniversaries are always difficult.'

'He could be awkward, everyone knows that – but he was my friend.'

'Yes. And friends matter.'

'My best friend, really – doesn't seem right. It just doesn't seem right.'

'No. Well, it isn't. There's nothing right about it.'

'We had this secret language. Special codewords that only we knew...'

For new things to grow, we all need to speak our hurt without fear or judgement. But the supermarket is too insecure about itself to acknowledge the pain of another. It wants to move on, be positive; talk prawns or talk balls – whatever it takes to distract. Who wants to hang around pain? Get over it! In the meantime, it's accepting no responsibility and no blame.

And will anyone take responsibility for Toad? Don't bank on it.

Toad is a recent arrival from another store. He is thirty-eight going on seventy; has been with the store since the invention of the wheel, and comes with the reputation of being 'an induction specialist'.

'You can leave it to me now,' he says, rolling up his sleeves, as though he's a craftsman or something – when in fact he's just prematurely dull. 'I'll take the young'uns through their paces. Been doing it for years.'

'Been doing it badly for years,' says Caspar, after he leaves the canteen. 'Have you heard him?'

And sadly, later in the day, I do – I witness the King of Induction at work, with a young new employee called Owais. We are about to find out just how much 'obvious' a man can take:

'This is the front door,' says Toad, standing by the front door.

'Yep,' says Owais, for there isn't a lot else to say.

'Place of general access, during the day, for staff and customer alike.'

'Yep.'

'Busy thoroughfare, as you'd expect.'

'Yep.'

'And particularly dangerous – *when?*'

'Sorry?'

'When might this door be particularly dangerous?'

Owais is caught out.

'Er – I don't know.'

'Well think, boy – when might an entrance suddenly turn nasty?'

'When a suicide bomber walks in?'

'When *wet*,' says Toad. 'A doorway is particularly dangerous when wet. It's not wet today, clear blue sky, with very little cloud – but it could be wet on another day. You can never tell with the weather.'

'Nope,' says Owais. 'Although it's not just the weather. You can never tell with anything, can you? Nothing is certain.'

'All you need to know for our purposes is that in heavy rain, this door can become a death trap.'

'Right.'

'Note also the fire extinguisher,' says Toad, pointing down to his left with some drama.

'Yep.'

'That's in case of fire.'

'Well there's a thing.'

'Sorry?'

'Nothing.'

'So any questions thus far?'

'About what?'

'About anything – the door?'

'Nope.'

'You've logged all that then?'

'Yep.'

'When's it dangerous?'

'When wet.'

'Smart lad. And the fire extinguisher – familiar with those, I expect?'

'Yep.'

'Good. Standard model, of course, in the traditional red – only to be used in emergencies obviously.'

'Yep.'

'You don't want to be setting it off accidentally.'

'Nope.'

'Or there's merry hell to pay.'

'I'll remember that.'

'I once saw a young lad blinded by a fire extinguisher.'

'Really?'

'Thought he was a comic, he did – and perhaps he was. But now he's a blind comic.'

'That's a great shame.'

'His choice.'

'Well, hardly a choice.'

'Oh – someone forced him to play the fool with the extinguisher, did they?'

'I didn't say that.'

'They told him to do it, I suppose?'

'All I'm saying is – he didn't choose to be blind.'

'He chose to play the fool – same thing.'

'No, I'm sorry, but it's not the same thing.'

'Same thing in my book.'

'If every fool was struck blind – then no one would have

their sight. It's all a bit more random than you suggest.'

We didn't know it at the time, but Owais is a philosophy student – and before coming to this country, had spent two years up a mountain in Nepal at a Buddhist monastery. But Toad is moving on. He has an induction to finish.

'So that's the main entrance,' he says, cradling his clipboard like the Madonna and child. He turns back into the shop. 'Follow me, because we're now moving across the store – calmly at all times – towards the *back* door, which is a rather different kettle of fish. Have you used the back door?'

'I came in by it this morning.'

'Of course you did. Staff access before the store opens. Well done. Any problems with it?'

'Nope. Pretty traditional door as I remember…'

I later apologised to Owais for his induction experience.

'Does he always do it?' he asked.

'Yes, he does – unfortunately.'

17.

DEAD MEN'S SHOES

In which Sapphy discovers that friends
can be murder, and Simon tries
Mohammed's shoes. A funeral visit is
remembered, Rosemary has wedding
plans, and Simon is shocked by some
extraordinary gymnastics.

It's early morning, and I find Sapphy alone in the store by the newspapers. She is upset, and with more reason than sometimes. She is normally upset because she is bored, or the vending machine isn't working, or because she wants to do something else but doesn't know what, or a mate is 'treatin' her all funny'. Today, however, she is upset because her friend has been murdered. She knew Shak at school, but two nights ago, he was out for a drink when a scuffle broke out in the street, and he was stabbed in the neck – stabbed repeatedly. The attacker disappeared, and Shak was dead on arrival in hospital.

'I carn work today, Si – no way! Shak's bin knifed – and I only saw 'im a monf ago!'

'And he was a good bloke?'

'Yeah – well friendly, ee was! Everyone liked Shak.'

'It's terrible.'

Sapphy then gave her views on what should happen to the

murderer. 'Ee shouldn't be allowed to live. People like vat – vey shouldn't be allowed to live.'

I leave her by the magazines, with the solace of OK!, and go to the canteen where I am met by Mohammed. He wants me to have his shoes.

'You take these shoes,' he says.

He has just put his lunchtime curry in the fridge, and is now offering me a fairly new pair of shoes, which he explains do not fit him. 'They are for you – or you will have the managers down your back again.'

'On my back again, that's the phrase.'

'What?'

'I'll have the managers on my back again.'

'I don't see how they can be on your back?'

'Only if you lie down,' says Caspar.

'And that isn't going to happen,' I say hastily.

It is true what Mohammed says, however. The managers have recently been saying that my beige shoes are not welcome on the shop floor. Like undertakers and priests the world over, we are meant to wear black shoes on duty – and the shoes on offer now are as dark as the night. So should I take them?

They say that love is the ability to stand in the shoes of another. This is particularly true when you don't actually like their shoes, and this is where I am with Mohammed's. Were I choosing shoes for myself, I would not choose these. And there are other factors to consider. Sure, my shoes are cheap beige suede. But really, when you start looking around and down, few other people's shoes were entirely black. Caspar, for instance, wore black trainers with a cool white stripe; Faith's footies are definitely dark blue, while for the last week or so, Sapphy has been wearing a pair of what are basically red silk slippers. She looks very nice in them; like someone fresh from Aladdin's cave. But they are a long way from black, as are Waheed's green plimsolls and Ayub's mildly orange clogs. It was like at school. Everyone with the same uniform – and no one dressed the same.

I decide to give Mohammed's shoes a road test on the shop floor, and Faith clocks them straightaway.

'Aren't those Mohammed's?' she asks.

'Er, yes – he gave them to me,' I say. I didn't want her thinking I'd knocked him out and stolen them – leaving him bound, gagged and shoeless by the crisps.

'You should never wear other people's shoes, Simon.'

'Well, they're my shoes now.'

'No, that is not my point. He's worn them. It's about health and safety.' Well, why not? Everything else seems to be.

'My biology teacher told us,' says Faith. 'Once a shoe moulds to someone's foot, it's dangerous for another to use that same shoe.'

I thank Faith for her borrowed wisdom, and find myself remembering a visit I made as a priest to the breathless and lacquered Elizabeth Fagg. I had buried her husband Albert earlier in the week, but when I went round to see her on Thursday, she had only shoes on her mind.

'What size do you take?' she asked on my arrival.

'Sorry?'

'What size do you take – in shoes?'

'An eight.'

'You're a similar size to Albert.'

'Well, he was a little taller, I think.'

'But his shoes would fit you. He had some nice shoes, he did. And some shirts he'd hardly worn. You could take them with you today.' And save her a trip to the charity shop, no doubt.

'That's very kind, but I'm fine thanks.'

She wasn't to be put off, however, and we were soon upstairs in her bedroom, wardrobe doors flung wide, and a vast array of shoes before us. 'Bert never understood why I needed quite so many shoes!' she said. 'He just didn't get it.'

I was struggling to get it as well. But there to the left of the Imelda Marcos collection of footwear, were four pairs of shiny men's shoes.

'Try them,' she said.

I was looking at some shoes I didn't want – shoes I wouldn't have worn, even if they were a personal gift from Nelson Mandela.

'Size tens,' I said, with some relief.

'Try them anyway, Reverend – they could be a small ten. And I'm not asking anything for them...'

Memories! And back in the canteen, Rosemary arrives for her break in the most dainty of shoes. I clearly have heightened awareness. Previously, whole years have passed without me giving shoes a thought; now I see them wherever I turn.

'Hello, gorgeous,' says Rosemary.

'How are you? OK?'

Rosemary is wearing thick gold eye shadow today, which looks stunning on her black skin. She sits herself down and grabs my arm. 'We should go on holiday together. Where do you fancy?' I hesitate, and she comes in quickly, 'Only joking of course! I have too many essays to write! But I must meet your dad. Can I meet your dad? I bet he's a truly wonderful man. Yes?'

Despite doing my best to avoid her, she has been all over me for the past few weeks, and you can only hide behind the root vegetables for so long.

'You'll have me walking down the aisle one day!'

'*Aisle* be the judge of that.'

'Oh, you and your jokes! I'll still marry you.'

But before our wedding of the century, she wants me to write an essay for her.

There is a slight history to this request. I have sometimes helped people with their CVs, and recently wrote a letter to the local council on behalf of two staff members with unjust parking tickets. Both had their fines rescinded, and this success brought other job offers my way. I was now having to rethink my whole work/life/writing-other-people's-essays-for-them balance.

'Here's the title,' she said.

She showed me some meaningless words, which turned out to be a sociology assignment from her evening class. Sociology is well known as the study of those who don't need to be studied by those who do, and frankly, a lifetime of poverty, chastity and obedience was preferable to getting entangled in this nether-world of human analysis.

'I just need you to write me two thousand words by Monday,' she says.

'I'm not going to write it, Rosemary. I have other things to do.'

'You wrote Betty's.'

'I didn't write Betty's. I just gave her some outlines.'

'Then give me some outlines.'

'I don't have the time. But I'll read through anything you do.'

Rosemary applied lip gloss to her full but disdainful lips. My answer had not been the correct one, and it was clearly time to take Mohammed's shoes back onto the shop floor.

I had shelves to stack, tills to operate – and perhaps wedding plans to cancel.

Mohammed hates Rosemary, and as is the way of things, wants others to hate her too. There is dark pleasure in shared dislike, and the shop floor remains a hotbed of shifting alliances as enemies change and new needs arise.

'Rosemary was looking for you,' he says.

'She found me.'

'What did she want?'

'She wanted me to write an essay for her.'

'She's a lazy bitch.'

'Not with her make-up.'

'She does no work on the shop floor; and now she wants you to do her schoolwork! My God!'

'Oh well – I suppose we're all looking for favours.'

'She's a manipulator.'

This was true. Rosemary did tend to mimic a cat – either purring round your ankles or ignoring you completely. But feelings of enmity are best allowed to pass through us, instead of being stored or shared with others – so I don't follow up Mohammed's remark. I like the story of the man who stood by the river. Upstream was a big tree, which occasionally dropped its leaves into the water. The leaves would then float downstream past the man, and as they did, he would place on each one any disturbing or aggressive thoughts he had – and watch them float away.

We are not made ill by brief thoughts. We are made ill by thoughts allowed to stay.

But I must close by returning to Sapphy, for there was a twist in the tale of today's shocking news. Three days after the murder of Shak, an arrest was made, and an individual charged.

Sapphy should have been delighted – but she wasn't. The murderer's name was Dion, and it turned out that Dion was an even better friend of Sapphy than Shak. And so she was now changing her tune.

'We was at primary school togevaa, me an' Dion. We go way back. So I ain't condemnin' 'im!'

'Change of tune.'

'Nor really.'

'Well, you wanted the killer hanged on Monday.'

'So?'

'And now he just needs a bit of TLC?'

'We doan know what went on, do we?'

'You're saying he had his reasons for stabbing him in the neck?'

'Well, no offence or nuffin' – but Shak could be irritatin'.'

'Oh, that's all right then.'

'I mean, we doan know the 'ole story, Si – that's what I'm sayin'. You can't believe what you read in the press.'

'You do most days.'

'An' I tell ya – Dion's mum is goin' ta be well upset.'

'Yes. Though I shouldn't think Shak's mum is holding a party either.'

I am staggered by the psychological contortions on display, as Sapphy turns the murdered into aggressor. She jumps from one absolute to another, and I sense even she feels uncomfortable with her mental gymnastics. She becomes defensive and bullish.

'That's the way it is, Si. Loyal-ee. An' I doan care what you sii; I doan care! Ee was my mate. Not goin' ter say nuffin' 'gainst 'im.'

Strange, but on this occasion, I find myself more disturbed by Sapphy than Dion.

18.

COURT IN THE ACT

In which news of an in-store burglary
becomes common knowledge, despite
Pinocchio's smoke and mirrors. But who
is the thief? A surprise twist of events
leads Simon to Head Office.

Ooh-er!

There is shock news as we stagger in for the morning shift. After our burglary a few weeks ago — when allegedly two members of staff not only counted the takings, but also took them home — Burglar Bill has struck again! Only this time, there were several 'Bills', they all wore masks, and apparently kidnapped Bryn to gain access to the shop after hours. There is talk of something over £15,000 going this time.

'I saw this programme on lawless Britain,' says Garry as we put our lunch in the fridge. Mine is the usual home-made sandwich and apple, to be eaten later sitting on the bench by the town hall.

'Good?'

'Interesting. But I'm glad my mum wasn't watching. It was about the dark side of life. I mean, I'm not a prude, but this was way beyond the acceptable boundaries.'

'You must understand — I needed the money.'

'No seriously, Si — I tell you, there's some lowlife out there.'

'"We lift the stone that is Britain today – and see what crawls out!"'

'I tell you, I'm not staying in this country any longer than I have to. I'm making plans. Go to Greece or something. I've got a mate there – I could get work there in a bar.'

'So was Bryn injured or wasn't he?'

Pinocchio is playing secret squirrel, and telling us nothing. Gradually, however, as the day unfolds, we piece together events. Bryn is now at home, but was apparently tied up by the burglars. He eventually got himself free and raised the alarm. There are rumours that he was knocked about a bit, and then counter-rumours that he wasn't touched at all. This is the secret of legend making – the fewer facts the better, and preferably none at all.

By lunchtime, as more sources are tapped, it seems Bryn is in good physical health. The burglars apparently treated him well, leading to the suspicion that it may have been an inside job – the robbers knew Bryn, liked him and didn't want him hurt. This rumour spreads through the aisles like warm butter on toast, and suddenly we're all wondering the same thing: could it be someone here now – one of us? There's Mohammed, for instance. He desperately wants to leave his rickety staircase above the restaurant. Is this about his mortgage? Or Caspar? Perhaps he wants to run off with one of the Latvian massage girls from the sauna up the road. Garry, we know, wants a new life in Greece – but how far is he prepared to go to get it? You never know with people, and in a climate of suspicion, anything seems possible; and everyone a suspect. Even me. As far as I know, I was at home last night, watching the football. But now I'm beginning to wonder.

In fact, I'm about to hand myself in when an old lady approaches. Customers! On a day like this! It's too much, really! Can they not see we have other concerns? But there is a certain pleasure to be had, even here. Just as the management hate telling us anything, we love telling the customers everything. It makes us appear interesting for a moment – and helps pass the time.

'About fifteen thousand taken,' I say to the old lady.

'Really? Fifteen thousand?'

'They kidnapped one of the managers.'

'Kidnapped? Is he all right – or are they demanding a ransom?'

'I don't think so.'

'The problem comes when the ransom isn't paid.'

'Can be difficult, yes.'

'I wouldn't like a meat hook in the chest,' she says.

'A meat hook?'

'Not at my time of life, dear.' She was clearly a keen student of the dark side, but was going to be disappointed.

'He's fine, we think. He's been sent home to recover.'

'Oh.'

'But still frightening,' I say reassuringly. 'Helpless in the hands of serious crooks. Imagine it! Anything could have happened.'

The old lady's eyes are alight with wonder. She is imagining it, and glad to be doing so. It is perhaps as near as she'll get to lawless Britain this week, and she's making the most of it.

The police are in and out pretty quickly, but over the coming days we get a more sinister visit. Who are these nameless figures inhabiting the shadows and doing their business behind closed doors? It's the company's own security team – here to question everyone involved in any way. Key witnesses are spoken to; the whole store is scanned. They move around like tigers in the long grass; they say nothing, see every-thing, and then they are gone, as quietly as they came.

'Glad they're gone,' says Garry. 'Give me the heebie-jeebies, they do.'

But what now? Well, Bryn comes back to the shop for a few days. He answers questions rather vaguely, but perhaps he just wants to forget about it all; he certainly seems well enough. His hair is still gelled; his tie knot still enormous and he is keen to catch up on the gossip. In fact, things are quietly returning to normal when suddenly he is given extended leave.

Pinocchio says this is for Bryn's own safety.

'Look, guys, it makes sense. After all, he is a crucial witness in this case.'

The clear inference is that there are death squads adjusting their sights on Bryn even as he speaks – but Pinocchio's words pass over our heads. No one believes anything he says, even if he tells them the time. And they certainly don't believe him now. After all, this is a tinpot supermarket break-in; not a KGB defection. And as it turns out, it is a lie. There is no fear of death squads. Rather, Bryn has been suspended because as far as the shop is concerned, he is the key suspect. I learn of this when I am called to the phone one morning. It is Bryn.

'Hi, Si.'

'Bryn! How are you?'

'All right, mate, all right. But, er, would you represent me?'

'How do you mean?'

'At the hearing. I've got a hearing at Head Office, and I'm allowed a representative from the store.' His voice is strained. He is trying to keep up his one-of-the-lads swagger. But inside he's a scared little boy who's turned round in the crowd and can't see Mummy.

'Well, of course I'll represent you.'

'Cheers, mate. You'll be given the details. See you there.'

And that is that. I discover that the hearing will decide the case; decide Bryn's future. This is nothing to do with the police, but rather, is the shop's internal justice. How does it work? Do they have their own courtroom? I was soon to find out.

¤ ¤ ¤

As Coleridge, the poet, once told us: 'In Xanadu did Kubla Khan a stately pleasure dome decree.' And I'll tell you what – it probably looked a little like the building I now stand in. So this is Head Office? Wow!

I've seen the words printed on letterheads. I've even read of it in newspaper despatches, reporting on boardroom battles and financial downturns. Yet here I am now, little ol' me, within its generous arms – and lured by the ample array of slick coffee dispensers and wafting executive aftershave. Truly, this is some way from tantrums on the till, or the smell of rat's urine by the dustbins. Here, people glide from sales meeting to sales meeting, pausing only to consider more favourable pension schemes. Here are those who have left the shop behind, and who visit the shelves now only when absolutely necessary – with dapper suits and a patronising smile for those poor little people who still work there.

'I remember my first store!' they say, imagining we're interested, but in truth, it's a fading memory. They are corporation people now, and customers – merely 'footfall' on a print-out.

I feel myself seduced by the pleasure dome, but come to my senses just in time. I am here to ensure Bryn gets a fair hearing, and refuse to sell my soul for a cup of posh coffee and a ride in an executive lift.

The defendant is a huddled figure on the corporate sofa, with his trademark tie and white socks looking a little out of place. It was fine on the shop floor, but here? Well, I'm not sure it's quite the done thing. Executives don't wear white socks to work.

'When are we on?' I ask.

'She'll be back in a minute.'

'Who's "she"?'

'It's Denise.'

'Denise?'

'You know, the commercial manager who visits the shop sometimes.'

Ah, now I remember Denise. Only the last time Bryn described her to me as we stood by the salads, he had called her 'the bitch with the nice arse'.

'She doesn't like me,' he added, and I do remember her being less than impressed with Bryn's spiky hair. Yet this woman now holds his future in her hands, and the socks could be a problem.

'Is it just her?' I ask. 'I'd imagined a panel or something.'

Well, to be honest, I'd imagined a courtroom and a wig, but I must hide the full extent of my disappointment.

'No, just her, I think.'

And so it is. We are led away from the marbled halls, down long corridors, and ushered eventually into a small and functional side room – the sort used by lesser executives for dull Power Point presentations. And here the investigation is led not by Morse, Columbo or indeed Kay Scarpetta, but by a commercial manager called Denise, who is famous only for being a snob – if a snob with a nice arse.

'You can only ask questions of clarification,' she says to me curtly, as we sit down.

Message received. She doesn't want me here, and out go any ideas I may have had of John Grisham-esque speeches to the jury. There is no jury – just Denise. And I don't think she likes either of us.

Of course, the main question of clarification I want to ask is this: 'Why on earth are you handling this matter? Who are you to be doing what you're doing? What qualifies you? Why are you here?' Those questions cover most of the bases.

Bryn's basic story is that he came off duty, went to the pub, and was then waiting at a bus stop when he was surrounded by a gang. They threatened him with a screwdriver, and told him to go with them. They put him in the back of a car and drove him to the shop, where they made him open up. He then let them into the office, where they cleaned the place out and left him tied.

Denise's basic story is that Bryn is lying, and that he colluded with the thieves. We watch some of the TV footage. It is odd to watch Bryn suddenly appearing in the darkened shop and walk slowly up the aisle. I have to say he looks pretty relaxed. The gang follow him thirty seconds later.

'Help me out here, Bryn,' says Denise, sucking on her biro, like puzzled detectives do on telly. 'Why didn't you ring someone on your mobile or set off the in-store alarm? It seems to me you had more than one opportunity.'

'We're always told not to risk our personal safety,' says a robot-like Bryn. This is true – you may remember that they were furious when I chased a thief.

'I reckoned I'd be doing just that, if I sounded the alarm,' he continues.

'To be honest, Bryn, I'm having a little trouble with your story at this point,' says Denise. 'Run it past me again, would you? And don't be nervous. I want the truth as much as you do.'

I think I heard those exact lines in an episode of *Heartbeat* a few weeks back. Or was it *Midsomer Murders*? Whichever, it is reassuring to know we are in safely scripted hands. But in the end – with no evidence, apart from the evidence of circumstance – you either believe Bryn or you don't. And Denise clearly doesn't. Indeed, it is clear the case was decided long before we entered the building this morning; I feel the clammy hand of the in-store security team in the background. I point out to Denise that she has no evidence for her assertions, but then this isn't a criminal court – it's a retail court, and the rules are different. The rules of a retail court are surprisingly similar to those of the kangaroo variety. Bryn is sacked on the spot.

We part company on the Underground.

'See you around then,' I say. 'And good luck.'

'Don't need it, mate, don't need it. I'll see you around.'

But we don't see him around. Or hear from him – he never answers his phone or returns calls. My last memory is of him stepping from the Tube at King's Cross, and out into the encircling gloom.

The police never found the robbers – but equally, they never considered Bryn a suspect.

19.

THE BOOK OF
OUR LIVES

In which Brian's book-writing gives a literary flavour to our canteen lunch. Sapphy likes the idea of writing a book, if she could think of something to write about; while Winston looks only to the end of the world — and the bonfire of vanities.

Brian, our in-store witch, is writing a book. Every day after work, he returns to his lodgings, pens a page or two and seems pretty proud about it all.

'I've been working on it for some time,' he says.

As he has raised the subject, I assume it's not only OK to ask questions but even polite to do so. 'A book? Wonderful! So what's it about?' I ask.

'Ahhh!' he says, and then leaves such a long pause that I wonder if he's dead. He moves slowly at the best of times – and stands very still now. He isn't dead, as it happens. But for whatever reason, he just doesn't want to tell me what his book is about – and pestering him has no effect at all.

'So do you write in your room?' I continue.

'Yes.'

'Looking out of the window?'

'Sorry?'

'Do you write looking out of the window? Isn't that where writers are meant to look for inspiration?'

'Er, well...'

It seems he wasn't sure if he looked out of the window. Or, perhaps he's just blanking me again, deeming this to be too much information. Good luck to the journalist sent to interview him on the publication of his masterpiece. They'll be fortunate to get his name and birthplace.

'So you aren't disturbed by all the screams and cries for mercy?' I ask.

I remember his home features an active dungeon.

'Cries for mercy are no different from the sound of traffic really,' he says.

'You must live on a different road to me,' I say.

'What I mean is — you get used to it.'

'Oh, I see.'

'And frankly, better a scream than hip-hop coming through the walls.'

Good point, well made.

🛒 🛒 🛒

Meanwhile, in the canteen, news of Brian's book-writing adventures becomes the talk of the canteen.

'You're rii'in' a book, Brian?' exclaims Sapphy. 'Vat is so amaizin'!'

And with Brian's domestic set-up well-known, links are made between the two.

'Will it be leather-bound?' asks Caspar.

'Chained to his writing desk,' says Garry. 'Whipping the story into shape.'

'Could be a great work of friction,' I add.

'We must just hope it doesn't get a caning from the critics,' adds Garry.

Oh, the mirth! But Brian remains impervious to it. No one knows what he is writing about, and he won't say, enjoying being a figure of mystery and the attention this brings. Sapphy, however, is not content with unknowing. If there is something to be known, she has a right to know it.

'You gor a tell us what it's all abart, Brii!' she demands.

Brian goes into one of his pauses again, but Sapphy doesn't allow it.

'So come on, Brii – tell uzz! What's your book abart?'

And behold the thaw! Suddenly, Brian is melting in the face of the feminine.

'Let's just say it's a saga,' he says with enormous pride.

'A saga?'

'A Viking saga set over three generations.'

Sapphy has got more from Brian in three seconds than I have managed in a year.

'That's all rape and pillage, isn't it?' says Caspar.

'And long boats,' adds Lottie, raising the tone a little.

'And IKEA's Viking, isn't it?' asks Sapphy.

Things are moving way too fast for Brian. 'The Vikings were Norsemen,' he says. 'Danes, Norwegians and Swedes who conquered large parts of this country around the ninth and tenth centuries – and were a very honourable people.'

'When they weren't raping you or pillaging.'

'Too much is made of that.' It does suddenly strike me that Brian looks a bit like a Viking. 'They've been part of the scenery here for a thousand years!' he adds.

'I did'un realise IKEA was that old,' says Sapphy.

Who's going to tell her? But before they do, Winston speaks: 'It seems everyone has to write a book these days. It's a national disease.'

'Izz nor a disease! I fink it's reelly good!' says Sapphy. 'I luv books!'

'So what would you write about, Winston – if you got the chance?' I ask.

'Me? I would never write a book. Like I say, it's a disease. Books are an entire waste of time. What is there to say which hasn't already been said?'

'There must be sumfing!' says Sapphy hopefully.

'You know the Book of Ecclesiastes, Simon,' continues Winston.

I nod.

'And what does it say? "In much wisdom there is vexation; and those who increase knowledge, increase sorrow. Vanity, vanity! All is vanity!"'

Is this the end of the book club? It's certainly a bit of a dampener. Faith vainly freshens up her lipstick, and Sapphy contemplates her fake tan, which looks very orange today. But me? I press on, feeling, not for the first time, that Winston knows the Bible better than I do – the depressed bits, anyway.

'But if you had to – if you had to write about something, what would it be?'

Winston peers through his thick glasses, and manages a smile: 'I'd write about the end of the world, and the complete destruction of everything.'

'Yeah – like anyone's goin' ter read vat!' says Sapphy. 'The end of the world? Not exactly 'appy, is it?'

'Would be for me,' says Winston. 'Very happy. And the sooner the better, as far as I'm concerned. Then we'd see.'

'See what?'

'See who was left standing – and who was taken away to roast.' Eternal torment is the last residue of religious belief in Winston; only hell remains. But just as he contemplates sweet vengeance on all who piss him off – starting with Sapphy – Pinocchio appears in the canteen.

There is no good reason for his arrival – other than to let us know that we've got five minutes left of our lunch break. He pretends to read a notice on the wall for fifteen seconds, and then turns to leave. Now that we know there's only five minutes to go (and we know that he knows that we know) he can disappear, which he does.

'It so gets on my nerves when he does that,' says Faith, turning briefly from her mirror. She's another one bound for eternal darkness in Winston's book. And on the subject of books, Sapphy is not quite done. 'I'd li'e to rii a book,' she says.

'Really?' I say.

'Oh yeah – I fink everyone's gor a book in them.'

'A shit book, maybe,' says Winston.

'Speak for yourself,' says our resident author, Brian.

'So what would you write about, Sapphy?' I ask.

'I dunno. That's the trouble, innit?'

'You need to have a theme really.'

'And all those words. So many bleedin' words. I dunno 'ow they do it, theeze wrii-arz!'

'And it's not just the number of words,' says Caspar. 'They all have to be in the right order as well.'

As the literary talk continues, I am reminded of an actor friend who agreed to do a performance at a charity event. He acted his socks off for forty-five minutes, after which the charity organiser – more at home with fund-raising than theatre – came up to congratulate him.

'Jolly well done,' he said. 'I don't know how you actors

remember all those words!'

It wasn't quite the critical acclaim he was looking for. 'And the Oscar for "Remembering all those words" goes to...'

And so ends another lunch break, which today has sounded more like a Writers' Support Group – without the support. But getting back to retail, there's a slight sense of deja-vu in the air. On our way back to the shop floor, we stop off in the Cold Store to collect and wheel out the morning stacks. These are the stacks we left there six hours ago – and it's time now to put on the shelves everything we couldn't put out earlier. I'm working the vegetables and salads with Brian, and hoping to hear more about the saga. Time can slow a little at this point in the day, and I'd love to discover more about the book.

The till bell rings – again and again and again. Someone is clearly angry, and no prizes for guessing who. It's Winston. On hearing the bell, we are meant to stop what we are doing and rush to provide reinforcements. Most staff become temporarily deaf, of course – but not Brian. He is till-bound immediately – an honourable Viking on a mission. He is back quickly, however.

'That didn't take long,' I say.

'There was no queue. Well, one person.'

'So why was the bell ringing?'

'It was Winston.'

'Ahh.'

Winston will often ring the bell for assistance, even if there is no one waiting.

'Better safe than sorry,' he says, pleased to have irritated us all just a little.

There may, as Ecclesiastes says, be much vexation in wisdom – but there's a fair amount in Winston as well.

THE SILENT BATTLE

In which Mavis and Leonard disagree,
and Simon sadly forgets a name.
We fight for the right to silence;
meet an advocate for polar bears,
and consider pay slips.

It was a casual question, really. Mavis and Leonard usually brought their son Jack with them, but I hadn't seen him of late. Jack was middle-aged, and a simple soul, who still lived at home.

'So how's Jack?' I ask expansively, as the sun shone through the window, warming my back by the bananas.

'He's dead,' says Mavis.

Had I misheard?

'Sorry?'

'He's dead.'

'Oh.'

'Well, wait on, Mavis,' says Leonard. 'He's not dead.'

'Ah?!' I say, cast afresh on a sea of unknowing. So how was Jack exactly? Dead? Not dead? I mean, heaven knows – couples disagree over many things, but this is not usually one of them. Perhaps Mavis has exaggerated slightly?

'Well, what is he then?' asks Mavis.

'He's passed away, dear,' says Leonard, determinedly

checking the pears.

'Oh,' I say. 'I'm – er…'

'He's dead, Leonard.'

'I prefer passed away, Mavis – it's less, well – you know… I mean how does young Simon feel?' He moves on to the oranges.

'I'm very sorry,' I say. 'I didn't realise– '

'Well, how could you? Funeral last Tuesday. Last Tuesday afternoon.'

'He doesn't need to know that!' says Leonard apologetically. 'I mean, he really doesn't need to know when the funeral was!'

'Vicar did us proud, I thought,' says Mavis. 'I mean Jack wasn't exactly the brightest spark … no, did us proud, he did. Spoke like he knew him. Didn't he, Leonard? Spoke like he knew Jack.'

'He was fine,' answers Leonard, in a manner that says only that none of this should be discussed.

I was glad the vicar spoke like he knew him, because it doesn't always happen. As a priest, I would always visit the family before a funeral, to get a sense of things – because no two deaths are the same. Only once in twenty years did I get a name wrong in the service. I went into the crematorium knowing it, but for some reason, another name came out of my mouth in the opening line. The family corrected me; I apologised profusely, and carried on. Once was enough with a mistake like that. I always felt an intruder at funerals anyway – a robed intruder maybe, but still an intruder on the grief of others. This blunder merely heightened that sense.

But it is Leonard who then asks if we'd be keeping a silence on Remembrance Day this year.

'I know you don't usually,' he says.

This was true, we never had before – but were things about to change? It was already something of a hot potato behind the scenes, and had so far proved – perhaps appropriately – a bit of a battle.

Pinocchio was against it because it had no commercial value. Remembrance is the only festival that supermarkets haven't yet been able to turn to their economic advantage – but hey, it's early days. There must be something tasteless on a drawing board somewhere. In the meantime, Pinocchio majors on the disruption to customers, as we discuss it at a team briefing.

'You all know they don't like being held up, guys.'

'So that's why all those people died,' I say, fairly furious. 'In the grand cause of unhindered consumption! And there was silly old me thinking it was about Hitler. Well, I'm glad no one died in vain.'

'I'm not saying that,' says Pinocchio carefully. 'Obviously the history is important, but, well, let's face it – we're running a store here, not a museum.'

'What?!'

'No, bur I mean, watz ver poin' reelly?' asks Sapphy, foursquare behind the manager. 'I mean, no offence, bur I doan geh all viss remembrance stuff. It was, lii, ages agow.'

'Still means a lot to a lot of people,' says Garry, whose young father fought in the war.

'Well, vey can orr remember it by vereselves – doan mee' we 'av to.'

'I don't believe in war,' says Caspar, in a moment of high earnestness, though I note he's also listening to his iPod.

'Well, I don't know what Winston Churchill would say,' tuts Brian, disturbed by events.

I was wondering which way he'd jump.

'Are we meant to be bothered?' asks Winston, happy to stamp on this icon of white England.

Things are changing. The white cliffs of Dover may still stand, but there's much of old England that doesn't. So would the proposed 11.00 am silence?

'Silence is about stopping the madness for a moment,' I say. 'It's good to stop sometimes. We remember the dead to say thank you to them across the years.'

'Lii vey can 'ear us!'

'Who knows? But if you don't want to remember the dead, if you struggle with that – remember the living. Remember yourself if you like. Remember who you are – and think who you want to be in the time left to you.'

There was a slight pause in the room.

'I doan mine remembrin' meesell,' says Sapphy.

Resistance to the silence melts – partly because of the new death-lite approach; and partly because no one wants to back Pinocchio. If he's against it, it must be a really good idea.

And when the time comes, it is Winston who is the star. He was in the middle of serving a customer, but when I gave the signal, withdrew his labour with something of a flourish.

'I am sorry, madam, but I am no longer able to serve you.'

'Don't be ridiculous.'

'We're remembering the brave dead, madam. Perhaps you'd like to join us?'

She's pretty exasperated – but of course, exasperation never deterred Winston. He may have no time for Churchill, but in that moment, showed something of his bulldog spirit.

There is initial panic in people's eyes, at the withdrawal of commercial normality. Some reach for their mobiles for reassurance – reassurance that not everything that gives life meaning has been withdrawn. It isn't about ringing anyone; just knowing that they can do if they need to; if the quiet all gets too much.

But slowly the fear goes, the silence takes hold, and proves rather wonderful. I stand in the doorway to discourage movement. One or two customers still gaze at the salads, making discreet lunch choices, but most take the opportunity to go, well – who knows where?

As for me, I am thinking about this little island that fought so bravely in the war – but presently feels so down.

So where to now?

🛒 🛒 🛒

Later in the day, and further adventures in remembrance – of polar bears. I am standing by the fish when a sharp-eyed old man approaches me, with some salmon in his hand.

'Where does this come from?' he asks.

'Alaska,' I say, unable to refrain from adding: 'Like it says on the label.'

'Yes, I can see that – but *where* in Alaska.'

'Where in Alaska?'

How was I supposed to know exactly where the salmon hailed from? He'd be asking for its mother's maiden name next.

'Alaska is a big country,' he says.

'And the exact spot matters, does it?'

'It matters if you're a polar bear,' he says.

'Because?'

'Well, this is their lunch, isn't it? This is what they'd be eating now, if it wasn't sitting here!'

'I suppose so.'

'I know so.'

I am weak on polar bears, but my inquisitor clearly knows enough for the both of us. 'Hence my question: where in Alaska does the fish come from?'

'Well…'

'I need to be sure it's from approved fishing grounds.'

'Oh, I'm sure they are approved.'

'There's an increasing amount of unapproved fishing.'

'We're pretty hot on everything being approved here. I mean, all our eggs are free range.'

'Oh, that'll really help the polar bears!' He's rather tickled by that, and is irritating me now. Polar bears are not best served by sarcasm.

'I'm not saying it will help them…'

'They don't go to work on an egg, you know!'

'I'm just saying that as a store, we take the environment seriously.'

'Yet you don't know where the salmon is from?'

I take a deep breath. 'I know the country – but not the postal code.'

My questioner shakes his head in amused self-righteousness. 'Ignorance is no defence in a court of law,' he says, before taking himself and his international concerns out of the shop, and down the road.

I return the salmon to the chiller cabinet, thinking only of a cold and hungry polar bear. I'm not sure which is harder: remembering the dead – or the living?

🛒 🛒 🛒

Often at the close of the day, I am with the potatoes. I like to pile them high before leaving, and imagine them steaming on people's plates tonight. Mashed? Boiled? Roast? Fried? Or in their jackets – with grated cheese and beans? Ahh! Endless mouth-watering possibilities! Anyway, Mohammed finds me here, with a complaint about his pay slip. It's the old grouse – that extra hours worked have not been recorded there.

I acknowledge his irritation, but am not the best advisor. I don't understand the pay slips – and as a priest, never knew what I earned. It wasn't a secret or anything – just not an issue. I know when I started out, it was around £12,000 pa, but after that, I lost track of it over the years. My guess is that it was around £17,000 pa when I left, plus free housing. It was always there, and always enough, as long as I was careful.

So although no one would become a clergyperson for the money – that's a joke! – they do earn a lot more than supermarket workers, when the free housing is taken into consideration. Some will say that's only fair, because they have a lot more responsibility – and certainly a parish is a big show to run, requiring both goodness and skill. But responsibility? That's all in the mind, I suspect; something that doesn't exist beyond our imaginations. There is just today – and the small things put before us. The president and the potato pile-er are equally responsible; or to put it another way, equally care-free. The president must run a country; and I must make sure the King Edwards do not end up with the Maris Pipers. And reassure Mohammed that I will take up his concerns with the accounts people.

'You will not forget?'

'I will not forget.'

Every day is remembrance day.

21.

WHEN TIME STOOD STILL

In which the Christmas party is
remembered and Dilip's disciplinary
hearing gets under way. It's last-
chance saloon for Dilip, and Simon is
his brief — unlike the proceedings.
But which way will it go?

You find me sitting with Dilip in a disciplinary hearing. It's not the first time I've represented him — and may not be the last. He is a slightly simple individual, famous particularly for the impromptu exposure of himself at last year's Christmas party, since when he has been called 'Pencil'.

The party need not detain us long. It was a karaoke evening in a local pub, and Bryn gave me Queen's 'Bohemian Rhapsody' to sing. I left with new respect for Freddy Mercury's vocal range, which apparently I failed to match.

'That man was a god, Si,' said Garry, who has all his music. 'And you were shit.'

Sapphy was kinder in tone, but similar in content. 'It did sarnd a bit, lii, ropey, Si. No offence.'

I thought I'd done pretty well, but as T.S. Eliot nearly said, 'This is the way the world will end, this is the way the world will end, this is the way the world will end, not with a bang but with rubbish karaoke singers, imagining they've got a voice to die for.'

And as I say, the other thing I remember from the evening was Dilip's genitals being waved for public view from a table in the corner, when alcohol had a disinhibiting effect on him.

But that was then. Everything's where it should be now, and we are sitting in the managers' office, all filing cabinets and sales targets. Dilip sits on a wheelie office chair, his stomach wedged tight into his shirt. His weight changes according to his inner state. There was a time last year when he was getting down to the gym, and looking much the better for it. If he's getting down there now, he's not getting past the canteen – and stopping off at the pub on his way home. It's alcohol that has brought us to this hearing.

'Do you think you have a drink problem?' asks the manager.

I'm immediately concerned. If we're going to list all of Dilip's problems, we could be here for some time.

'No!' says Dilip, with inappropriate vigour – like a child who has just learned the word, and is keen to show it off. 'No!'

'But you've been coming into work drunk.'

'Not so, my friend, not so!'

Dilip's defence is courageous, but untrue. He's always coming in drunk.

'Are you saying you haven't been drinking before coming into work?'

'What I do in my own time is up to me.'

'Not if it makes you unfit for work.'

'I am not unfit for work. Who said I'm unfit for work?' His shirt is bursting with sweat and indignation.

'We can smell alcohol on your breath, Dilip – when you come in.'

'Could be anything. I'm on medication.'

'Really? Well, I'd be interested to know what you are taking.'

'I'm sure you would!' says Dilip, like he's in one of those dull middle-England sitcoms, and looking for laughs.

'You have been behaving in a drunken manner.'

'I don't know what you mean,' he says, and then turning to me, 'Si – what's he talking about?'

Dilip's poor sense of self postures like a peacock in the early afternoon – and is painful to listen to. Although I'm representing Dilip, I'm not without sympathy for the manager. What should he do? If this was an episode of *The Bill*, he'd say: 'Take him back to the cells, Sergeant. We'll let him sweat a bit.'

But it isn't *The Bill* – it's *The Supermarket*, where exile to the tills is as tough as it gets. And Dilip sweats all the time anyway, so there'd be nothing new there. Neither is Dilip following his brief's advice. Before the meeting, I had suggested to him that it might be best just to say sorry; to make a clean breast of things, and be a little contrite. 'A fresh start and all that.'

'I don't need a fresh start, Si – I haven't done anything wrong.'

A drunk colleague has few friends; and a drunk colleague in denial has none. But who knows? Perhaps this can be his zero hour, when new algebras of being are created? Perhaps this crisis is a severe mercy, when beyond known remedy he sees through to the light. In my experience, humans don't seek inner renewal without pressing and compelling reasons. Things have to be pretty bad before we let go of old and discredited ways – but were they now bad enough for Dilip?

'I think the management would be sympathetic, Dil – if you were honest. And Stav likes you – he always puts in a good word.'

'I don't need any good words, Si. I haven't done anything wrong.'

It is at this point that something in me dies. 'Dilip, you were drunk, abusive to a customer – and then fell forward on the till unconscious, reeking of whisky.'

'Whose side are you on, Si?'

The next day we are back for the second part of the investigation, but there's a difference – in this session, everything has to be recorded. So while our manager asks the questions, another – Stav – has to act as scribe. And like thick treacle going up stairs, it's all very slow. I use a calendar to keep an eye on the time.

'Just repeat what you said, Dilip,' says the manager. 'So Stav can get it down.'

'What?'

I'm not sure Dilip is particularly aware of where he is, who he is, what he's doing, or why he's doing it. Apart from that, he's pretty focused.

'Simply repeat to me what you just said,' says the manager. 'We have to write it down verbatim.'

'What's that then – furbaitin?'

'*Verbatim* – it means word for word.'

'Swallow a dictionary or something?! What do you reckon, Si?! Reckon he swallowed a dictionary?!'

I smile supportively.

'So just repeat what you said,' says the manager, wilting a little. 'And then we can get on, which I'm sure we all want to do.'

He's sick of Dilip. If it wasn't for Stav's support, he would have sacked him last year. For some reason, Stav has a soft spot for him. If the manager has a soft spot for him, it's probably some quicksands near Dover.

'What I said when?' asks a confused Dilip.

'Just now. What you said just now.'

The centuries are flying by.

'I don't know what I said,' says Dilip after some reflection.

'You were talking about what happened on the till.'

'Oh yeah.'

'So?'

'I can't remember exactly what I was saying.'

'But the gist of it.'

Dilip looks as blank as a blackboard in the school holidays.

'It doesn't matter if you want to put it another way,' says the manager with a sigh.

'Why doesn't Stav just put down what he thinks I said?' suggests Dilip.

'We can't record what we think you said. We have to have a record of what *you* said. That's the whole point of all this.'

It was good to be reminded of the whole point of all this, for I was drifting a little. I was even beginning to read the 'commercial targets' poster.

'Yeah, but I can't remember what I said. What did I say, Si?'

'You were talking about the tills, Dilip; about what you said to the customer.'

'Oh yeah.'

'You were saying you weren't rude to her.'

'Yeah, that's it, that's it. I wasn't rude. There's no way I was rude to that woman. She has a problem, I tell you. Big problems – you ask her. There's no way I was rude to that woman!'

'Hang on, hang on,' says the manager. 'You're talking too fast. Stav has to write all this down, remember – so don't say anything new until we've got down what you said before.'

Stav looks up from his scribbling. 'Presumably I don't need to record the bit about not saying anything new?' he asks.

Eternity staggers on with Dilip denying all responsibility. But then, in a way, he has been well taught. This is a store which denies all responsibility – remember we are forbidden to apologise to customers, or use the word 'unfortunately'. Such things give the impression we have let the customer down, which is something we can never admit to, or the sky might fall on our heads. So Dilip's not admitting to anything either.

We are both asked to leave the room, while the manager and Stav consult. We sit together in the canteen, but struggle for conversation. After five minutes, we are invited back, to hear that Dilip has been sacked. He is shocked, and seems to blame me as we return to the canteen.

'We should appeal.'

'We can't appeal.'

I doubt this is true. There probably are procedures to prolong this affair. But if the 'we' included me, then it was true. I couldn't appeal.

'I think it's time for fresh adventures, Dilip.'

'Washing your hands of me, eh, Si? Just like the rest of them.'

I find myself eager to be back on the shop floor, and dealing with good, honest vegetables. But Dilip beats me there, announcing the injustice to all who will listen, customer or staff.

'They've sacked me.'

'Really?'

'Yep. Sacked. And for what? For nothing.' He speaks with passion and power.

'So much for a fair hearing in this place. A fair hearing? No way! No fucking way!'

People are generally sympathetic to his cause, but Dilip hears only himself as he strides around the store, spilling his grievance. And not everyone is sympathetic.

'I'm so relieved,' says Faith. She has come over to find out what happened. 'I thought he was going to get off again. He leers at me untold!'

'Everyone leers at you, Faith.'

She giggles. 'Yeah, but he's fat and drunk and sweaty.' Faith is after a better class of leerer.

As for Dilip, he was offered the chance to go immediately, but worked his notice, up until the very last minute. He had no desire to be gone, and it was hard to see what would become of him now; what exactly he could do. Interestingly though, a month or two later, I was putting out the salads when Mohammed told me that Dilip was now doing very well as a mortgage consultant.

I laughed, but he was most insistent it was true. Who knows?

22.

THE MADDENING ASCENT TO POWER

Pinocchio's in the zone; Glyn's in a
panic; Faith's getting lippy and Simon's
under a till. Why oh why oh why?
The area manager is coming! A man
who has history with Simon...

Back in the tenth century BC, the Queen of Sheba visited the Hebrew monarch, King Solomon. She had heard of his great wisdom and journeyed from her Ethiopian kingdom with spices, precious stones and large amounts of gold. On arrival, Solomon reciprocated in some style, with gifts and 'everything she desired'. (The Bible can be a tease sometimes.) After a while, however, she went back to her own land, and I only mention all of this because, recently, the area manager travelled to see us – and if you remove the gold, precious stones, sex and wisdom from the story, it's not dissimilar. Oh, and obviously Ethiopia doesn't feature either.

You know the area manager is coming because even as you walk in the door, there are three managers on the shop floor, jackets off and perspiring freely.

'The area manager is coming today,' says Glyn, who has replaced Bryn after 'The Embarrassing Affair of the Stolen £15,000.'

Glyn is the spit of Bryn. Gelled spiky hair and thick knotted tie – he really could be his slightly spotty younger brother.

Meanwhile, Pinocchio puts out chickens with a missionary zeal. 'I want you lot on the shop floor immediately,' he says to us natives, without looking round. 'The area manager is coming today.'

This couldn't mean less to the staff – but does mean a lot to him. After all, he has a career to look after. He's not with Solomon in the wisdom department, but he can at least give the area manager 'everything he desires' in terms of presentation – and receive in return a good word in the ear of Head Office. As in the tenth century BC, so now – gifts are a reciprocal thing.

'It's very much the five Ps,' says Glyn.

'The five peas?'

'Perfect Preparation Prevents Poor Performance.' He'd clearly swallowed a training manual overnight, and was unwell.

'So when's he arriving?' asks Garry.

'Nine o'clock. So there's no slack.'

'The area manager – is he the prat in the suit?' I ask, seeking clarification.

'He's *a* prat in a suit,' says Caspar. 'But hardly the only one.' This is a fair point. A number of 'suits' do visit us with their dandruff, clipboards and patronising words. It's unfair of me to demonise the area manager in particular. 'We boast a wide selection of suited prats,' says Caspar.

Garry then starts to impersonate a David Attenborough voice-over for one of those nature programmes: 'And here, before our very eyes, and apparently quite unconcerned by our presence, is the Lesser-Gifted Suit Prat. And so far from home. He'll need to get back to his nesting grounds at Head Office by nightfall, but for the moment, happy enough it seems to strut and shit his way round the store. A truly remarkable sight!'

Meanwhile Glyn is having a go at Faith. 'This is not the time for lipstick,' he says.

'It's not lipstick,' says Faith. 'It's lip salve. There's a difference.'

'Not interested. You should have been on the bakery ten minutes ago.'

'And I will be.'

'What d'you mean, "You will be"? You will be there ten minutes ago? Have you got a Tardis or something?'

'I don't know why you're getting in such a state,' she says, continuing with her lips.

'Because the place is a tip, and it's a race against time!'

'Ooh! A race against time!' says Caspar, in camp fashion.

'It's like in that garden programme on TV,' I say. 'You know – they send the owners away on some false premise, and then have to change the lawn, add a pond, rip out the patio, and stick in a couple of garden gnomes before they get back.'

'Has this got anything to do with anything?' asks Glyn.

'Not really. It's just the presenter in that keeps saying "it's a race against time" – because if it wasn't, then really, who'd give a flying–'

'Look, this is not TV!' says Glyn. This is his first managerial post – and he's seizing it with both desperate hands. 'This is a real race.'

'It's no race from where I stand,' says Faith. 'The area manager means nothing to me.'

As ever, Faith has got to the nub of the issue. Sometimes it's good when things mean nothing to us; when social conventions or the expectations of others are not allowed to oppress us. As Socrates said: 'There's so much I have no need of' – which leads me to wonder if he too didn't work in a supermarket.

In the ascent of Everest, you begin to go mad after 17,000 feet. This is a fact. From then on, it's not about great feats of mountaineering; but about staying sane. Once you reach 17,000 feet, delirium strikes even the most experienced and fit climbers; from here, you need to get to the top, and back down again, as soon as possible. And what's true for mountaineering is true for the rest of life. The ascent to power is a maddening climb, leaving those at the top struggling to stay sane, and often quite unfit for purpose.

Take being a priest, for instance. The important thing about being a priest is never to take the Church seriously. You can have tremendous adventures with your community, as long as you never imagine that there is some higher ideal you are promoting. You believe in the possibility of people and the possibility of God. But what you don't believe in, if you wish to stay sane, is the institution of the Church.

This is not good news for a career, of course. If you want to get on in the Church, you will need to believe in it; you will need to talk about the institution like it matters. And that's the 17,000 feet moment – from here on, you start to go mad. I remember sitting with an old friend in a pub. I had left the Church, and he had remained, which was fine – but something in him had changed. Instead of sitting light to the game, he was taking it seriously, as though it mattered. Suddenly I was finding it hard to see the person behind the collar.

'You're starting to believe it,' I thought, in a state of sadness and shock. For I knew that once he had been different; that once he had been free.

Glyn is starting to believe it too – starting to believe in the organisation. And Pinocchio certainly is; he's staking everything on it. Pinocchio is an ambitious young man. He wants to climb the company ladder and manage one of the flagship branches – not the rowing boat he currently finds himself in. This is why he currently has me lying on my back, cleaning the underside of the tills.

'Could you give the underside of the tills the once-over, Simon?' he asks.

Somehow, I don't see the area manager dirtying his suit to check down here, but Pinocchio wants to cover all bases – and I'm up for the adventure.

The underbelly of the tills are easily missed in the course of the day, but once discovered, prove a wonderful world of metal, grime and insects – and one with its very own eco-system. I feel like Captain Kirk, boldly going where no one has gone before. It's so hard to find genuinely unexplored areas of the world these days, yet perhaps this morning, beneath the tills, I am doing just that. I half expect a desperate man to appear hollow-eyed and hairy from one of the dark corners I now clean – who, when questioned, turns out to be the last person to clean here. 'Agghh! Who are you?!' he screams.

'It's OK. I come in peace. I'm just cleaning before the area manager comes.'

'The area manager? Agghh!'

'How long have you been here?' I ask.

'You must go!' he shouts. 'You must go!'

'Please, calm down, calm down! Your work is done, my friend.'

'Done? It's never done! Mr Rooney said I must– '

'Peace. You must believe me – things have changed out there. The manager who sent you here is long gone.'

'Gone? Mr Rooney is gone?'

'Years ago.'

'You mean…?'

'Yes – he moved north to Rotherham, after he split from his wife. It's a man-boy called Pinocchio now. Mr Rooney is gone. You are safe to go back to your family.'

🛒 🛒 🛒

As it turned out, I had met the area manager before. It had been on one of those training conferences, run by HR. And towards the end of the day we had clashed.

It was a gathering of union chairs from the region. We had spent an interminable morning playing 'Get to know you' games – like this was important before we all went away and never saw each other again.

'Hi, guys!' said the woman co-ordinating the pretend relationships. 'I smell fun in the air, if you're all as mad as I am – which I strongly suspect you are!'

And really, it was downhill from there.

'Here's the plan! First, we want to get to know you; and second, we want to hear what you guys have to say about how we, as a company, should go forward!'

Two lies in one sentence! Marvellous. They wanted neither, of course. You must remember that in a supermarket, the workers are just the hands; the management are the only ones with heads. We were here today, as always, to be told what to do. And it was in the open forum that the area manager and I fell out.

'This is an open forum, guys – so be open!'

And so I was, raising an issue that had struck me as soon as I joined the company.

'I have only been with the company for six months,' I said with the deference required of a newcomer.

'No matter,' says HR. 'Fresh eyes. They're important.'

'Yes, I agree – and what strikes me as strange is that a worker who has been with the company for twenty years, putting in wonderful service – and I have someone in mind – is on exactly the same wage as a newcomer who has done only three months. I just feel it lacks – well, I don't know – imagination, I suppose. It feels a bit feudal, a bit like landowner and serf. It kills the human spirit – and I suspect loses the company a lot of good people.'

The area manager didn't say anything immediately, just staring into the middle distance. But in his summing-up, which was basically a chummy and self-justifying tale of his ascent in the business, he suddenly lost his cool, and went into a rant about 'certain people in the room who need to consider whether they want to remain with the company'.

The nervous glances in my direction from those around confirmed that it was my card being marked. Point made. But it was the coward's way – public denunciation rather than personal engagement; passive aggression which neither resolves nor creates.

I did stay with the company, though – and now nine months down the line, the area manager studiously avoids me when he visits our store. Somehow he's always looking the other way when near. But then fair's fair. I shouldn't think the Queen of Sheba spent much time with Solomon's cleaners.

23.

SEASONAL ADJUSTMENTS

In which the supermarket grabs
seasons old and new, to put a little
sparkle in its takings. Christmas?
Mother's Day? Teacher's Week?
Halloween? Valentine's Day? Whatever
the season, 'tis the season to make lolly,
tra la la la la, lala la lar!

The Church used to look after the major festivals, but super-markets do it now – and it isn't a charitable venture. Pinocchio's hands are thrust deep in his pockets as he tells me, with almost orgasmic excitement, exactly how much Christmas is worth. 'We take more in the three weeks before Christmas than we do in the following three months!'

Well, there we have it – proof that the story of a baby born in a stable on a magical night in Bethlehem still has meaning today. It's certainly getting Pinocchio excited.

'You can't argue with figures like that!' he emotes.

And you can't argue with the cash cow that is Mother's Day either. Mother's Day is a traditional festival of flowers, cards and chocolate. Supermarkets love to help with all that. But what supermarkets most like to help with is guilt. That's what really oils the commercial wheels.

'*She gave you your life,*' says the poster. '*What will you give her?*' And it works.

'I was finkin' of gettin' me mum chocolates,' says a depressed Sapphy, who probably doesn't like her mum. 'But I'm wondrin' if it'll be enuff?'

This is just what the supermarket wants to hear. Sapphy should be ashamed of herself for thinking chocolates would be enough. The mother god demands expensive presents if she is to be appeased – and the supermarket has some ideas...

ᗯ ᗯ ᗯ

'*Don't forget the most important person in your life!*' says another poster, and it is true in a way. Your mother's attitude towards you in your early years was a truly formative influence on your life, but whether you are grateful for that shaping is quite another matter. Indeed, you may feel you have spent the rest of your life recovering. Psychotherapists often say that the biggest problem for their clients is their inability to be honest about how they feel about their parents.

Jane in the store was treated appallingly by both her parents. Her father was still molesting her when she was in her thirties, and her mother turned the appropriate blind eye: 'That's just his way, dear.'

I ask Jane why she continues to try to please them.

'I suppose I'm still hoping they'll love me,' she says.

So people continue to tell their therapists that everything's fine with their parents – it's just the rest of their life that is a mess.

As a priest, I always struggled with Mother's Day. Some felt genuine warmth towards their mothers. But I would routinely counsel adults whose maternal experiences made traditional sentiments chokingly inappropriate. Never mind. The super-market's coming for you anyway – because guilt sells. Roses, cards and chocolates fly off the shelves, for the most important person in everyone's life. In the dictionary of supermarket profit, mum's definitely the word!

But supermarkets don't just steal festivals – they also invent them. Take Teacher's Week, for instance. Teacher's Week, at the end of the summer term, is the latest kid on the block and will soon make more money than Easter. It's a cracking commer-cial invention, whereby people are encouraged to say thank you to their teacher for being so wonderful – even if they weren't.

'You have to do it,' says one parent. 'Or how is the teacher going to treat Michael next year? It's like protection money, I suppose.'

Teachers can really clean up at this time of year, and super-markets want to clean up with them. Chocolates, wine, soap, candles and 'treat yourself' facials are the backbone to this par-ticular festival. And cards of course:

'Thank you to the best teacher on the planet!'

'Thanx to the teecher wot learned me!'

'This pupil now sees! Thank you.'

'Educashion is safe in your hands!'

'You're in a class of your own!'

Marvellous. You can't put a price on comedy, and you can't put a price on every parent buying a card and a gift in Teacher's Week. And talking of prices – because really, what else is there? – Halloween is now worth well over £100 million to retailers. Amazing really – for such a mish-mash of jiggery-pokery. But like the jackal in a drought, you take what you can in this business – and it's a quick and easy kill before the Christmas push.

All Hallows' Eve is both a pagan and Christian festival, when the spirits of the dead are supposed to return to their former homes. October 31 was the last day of the Celtic year, and so is particularly important for Brian, our resident witch. Yet surprisingly, while the rest of us are buying things scary and ghoulish – he isn't.

'For me, Halloween is about the passing of another year,' he says, as we put out yet more pumpkins. The pumpkins are really going very well this year.

'Not all the spooky stuff then?' I ask.

'Not at all.' There is a particular solemnity about his manner.

'So what will you be doing tonight?'

I knew what everyone else would be doing – trick or treating in alarming masks and haunting hats. But not Brian.

'Halloween is a time to look back on the year,' he says. 'It's a chance to name regrets, and to remember the departed.' He looks disdainfully at the pumpkins, pulls his ill-fitting trousers back up, and wanders off round the corner. I'm left reflecting that the only one not thinking of witches at Halloween is the witch.

Supermarkets, however, aren't so solemn. Halloween for supermarkets is a children's party around the theme of pointy hats and all things scary. The Halloween card market is thankfully under-developed, but there are plenty of chocolate figures wrapped in ghoulish silver foil, and a wide selection of devilish knick-knacks. Probably the bestseller is the fork used by demons for prodding people back down into the seething fires of hell when they try to escape: 'No freedom for you –

get back down! Down, down, down – back to the flames of eternal damnation!'

Only joking! This is all just for fun. Supermarkets don't do seething fires because that would be un-family; they just do the pretend forks and fun Satanic capes and horns. As always, they dip their commercial toes in the shallows of meaning. Easter is a bunny rabbit, Christmas, a flying snowman, and Hell, a jokey plastic prong. They love the fluff – but not the stuff.

Of course, there are always 'Halloween spoilsports' who complain. The spoilsports say we should sell goods less obsessed with darkness and despair – and this year, even a bishop joins in on the radio. The smooth supermarket spokesman makes polite work of him, however:

'We are sorry the bishop feels this way, but we are in the business to sell the kind of thing our customers want.'

And so say all of us! Give the public what they want! Indeed, why not go the whole hog, and erect gibbets in some of our larger stores for some Halloween hangings. History shows that hangings always get a crowd – just what the customers want. Maybe we could tie it in with a special offer. 'Attend two hangings – get one free!'

🛒 🛒 🛒

But don't imagine supermarkets are heartless – not around Valentine's Day, anyway. Valentine's Day is the first big festival of the supermarket year, and as the day approaches, you can't move for hearts. Chocolate hearts, hearts on cards and wait a minute – hearts on the sandwiches?

'Why the fuck have they got a heart on the tuna and sweetcorn sandwiches?' asks Garry. 'What's that about?'

'Must be the new food of love.'

'Food of love? You'll just be fucking fish breath.'

I think Valentine's Day is beginning to get to him, as are certain rumours currently doing the rounds. I don't want to descend into common gossip, but the fact is that some people think that Faith recently had sex with Caspar, so they are currently getting teased about this. Both seem very happy with the rumour.

'So did ya or didn't ya?' asks Sapphy.

Caspar just smiles a Mona Lisa smile.

'I wish they would tease me about having sex with Faith,' says Garry.

The original St Valentine was a Roman convert to Christianity, who was clubbed to death around 270 AD. The shops don't major on this; there are no club-shaped chocolates, for instance. But then the choosing of 'valentines' has nothing to do with the saint at all, being more closely related to the mating season of birds. Chaucer refers to this in his *Assembly of Fowls*:

'For this was on St Valentine's Day,

When every fowl cometh to choose her mate.'

🛒 🛒 🛒

I'm looking up at the sky. I stand in the doorway of the store, as autumn gives way to winter.

Seasons come and seasons go, and I love these grand time-keepers of our lives. 'This too will end,' they say, reminding us that nothing is for ever, and everything is now. They take no particular account of our needs. Summer, autumn, winter, spring – they may bless us, but they may also kill us. Being chancers all, we'll make our seasonal money, and grab what we can with our chocolate eggs, spooky masks and hearts on tuna rolls. But in the end, the seasons make us, giving then taking; everything becoming; then everything slipping away.

As I say, I'm looking up at the sky as winter takes hold. Seasons do not last long, and there's reluctance in my letting go, as the cold whips through my thin uniform. But all things must pass. Shoppers relax on arrival, glad to be out of the wind. And whatever the season, when I stop doing, and simply am, I know only that everything is perfect, just as it is.

24.

THE DAZZLING MASTER OF DISASTER

In which Vin talks business, and Manik gives a master class in how not to do things. We also meet Alesha, the prettiest girl in the world, and hear from Casanova.

Is Manik the worst deputy manager in the world? Probably. He spent his first team briefing telling us how great things were at his last store, and how terrible things appeared to be here. In terms of motivation, it was right up there with the death sentence, and he has struggled to gain a hearing ever since.

Manik tends to look after the evening shift – which is not the same as the morning. The morning staff are the boring ones, in a way. They tend to have families, get up before midday, and make attendance at work something of a priority. Not so the evening crew. They are the young ones, doing a few hours a week to fund their clubbing and their weed; or Asians seeking a foothold in the world of business. Take Vin, for instance, standing next to me on the till:

'So how are things?' I ask.

'Well, these are interesting times, Simon,' he says enigmatically. Something tells me he's not referring to the tills – so what does he mean? 'I am just investigating the possibility of starting a tile importing business, using authentic Indian materials.'

'Really?'

'Yes – the Indian side of the business is nearly sorted.'

'Will you need to move?'

'No, no – my father and brother will run that end. Though perhaps, in time, I will return.'

'When you've made your millions?'

'Nothing can be discounted,' he says with a smile. 'And then you must come out and see me when I do! It is very beautiful, my country.'

'Well, that would be wonderful.'

'Oh, and pray for me, Simon.' He puts his hands together in a gesture of devotion. 'I have my interview for the bank job next Tuesday.'

It is said with some truth of the evening shift that the students turn up if they are not drunk, and the Asians, if they are not meeting their accountant. But attendance on this shift has plumbed new lows recently, and the main reason is Manik, who suffers from DEAD – Deficient Emotional Awareness Disorder.

Manik is not without ideals. He has an ideal in his head of everyone doing something on the shop floor, and doing it very fast. This is his vision. It doesn't really matter what you are doing – as long as you are doing it quickly. What he doesn't have in his head is a sense of how humans thrive, or what actually needs doing. So on the morning after a turn by Manik, not only will there be some very specific suggestions in the suggestions box – the store will also look terrible.

Somehow, he reduces even the placid to violence. After hectoring a quiet young man called Shoab about getting a shelf filled, Shoab turned to Manik, and said in English, his third language: 'May you die childless.'

To some in authority, this would be worthy of note, but not for Manik. Like the Bouncy Dog in Noddy, he just brushes himself off and gets up again. 'Get that shelf filled now, all right?!'

He's not bothered about the whole childless thing. He just wants to see some action.

Whatever management mess he creates one day, he is back the next, bright as a button. Crisis? What crisis? He's a disaster imagining himself a success; a nightmare believing he's a dream – but above all, a skittle who won't stay down. Which, in a way, is quite winning – until you work with him, of course.

Manik finds it very hard to leave anyone doing a job. He gets suspicious if people take time or care. A rolling stone gathers no moss, as they say, and Manik feels he must constantly be ringing the changes. 'Stop that – do this instead!'

Free of charge, he graciously gives me a taste of his management philosophy. 'It's good to keep moving people, Simon,' he says – fresh and busy in his shiny grey suit.

'Why's that?' I ask.

It should be said at this point that for the good of the store, and the integrity of the human race, I have never acted on any instruction Manik gave me.

'Moving people about keeps everyone on their toes,' he explains.

'It doesn't keep anyone on their toes,' I say.

'I think you'll find it does.'

'No – it just gets them irritated; irritated they can't finish what they are doing. It's really very frustrating.'

'This is a lazy shop.'

'It's certainly a shop with poor morale.'

'I don't care about morale – I care about getting the job done.'

'But you don't get the job done.' I'm sorry, but it just slipped out.

'As I say,' says Manik, ignoring me, 'it keeps everyone on their toes.'

'And every job half finished.'

'Every job finished in half the time more like!' he says.

And with that, Manik takes himself off with a knowing smile.

As fresh complaints about Manik arrive almost daily, I decide to speak with Pinocchio, the store manager.

'How can I help you, Simon?' he asks warily.

'It's about Manik.'

Pinocchio again tells me that he is already taking action – but that managerial confidentiality does not permit him to explain what it is. 'Trust me, Simon. There are things going on behind the scenes.'

He is, of course, doing nothing behind the scenes, and there are good reasons for this. Manik is a soulmate for him in many ways. He is someone who mirrors Pinocchio's own restlessness and sense of separation from others. They both manage through suspicion rather than relationship. They each have plans for everyone, but not a heart for them. If Pinocchio were to criticise Manik, he would have to face the psychic fracture in himself, and that isn't going to happen.

So I approach Manik directly.

'How can I help you, Simon?'

He has turned down a private meeting in a room with a closed door. I think he would feel trapped. So we meet standing in the warehouse corridor.

'I think it's more about me helping you.'

'I don't need helping,' he says brightly, but the brightness doesn't quite reach his eyes, which show small traces of fear.

'I have had a lot of complaints about you.'

'If people complain, it's usually because I'm raising standards.' Manik has raised fewer standards than a pacifist – but such idealised perceptions are a necessary illusion for him. Some psychologists call it 'The buffer' – that remarkable part of our brain which maintains illusions we are not yet ready to lose. The human psyche can cope with very little reality, so our buffers work night and day to keep it out. From where he stands, Manik genuinely believes he is raising standards. He is vaguely aware of a shadow round the corner, suggesting another presence – but he can't name what it is; and he certainly isn't going to have a look. He senses danger there.

'Is there anything else to discuss?' he asks briskly.

'You could be a good manager if you listened to people,' I said.

'The salads need filling.'

I return to the shop floor feeling suitably repulsed, and find myself reflecting on the difference between the magnet heart and the rubber heart. Those with magnet hearts attract truth to themselves, from whatever source it comes. It is a rather humble affair, the magnet heart – loving to learn from all things. Rubber hearts are different. These are organs of resistance – tough, defensive and springy, and pushing all truth away. They can receive nothing, because they must insecurely oppose everything.

Like everyone, Manik could be a good manager – if he had the heart for it.

I'm gathering my stuff at the end of the shift. Today, I am eager to be away from neon light and promotional posters, and to feel instead the caress of the afternoon sun. I sign out, and then remember the cauliflower cheese I have stored in the fridge. I go back to the canteen and find everyone strangely gripped.

'Nice, eh?' says Caspar.

'Yep. I'm going to have it with fish fingers.'

'No, not the cauliflower cheese — *her!*'

'Jail bait,' says Garry.

'Is that like whitebait?'

'More dangerous; much more dangerous.'

In the canteen is a very pretty girl, new on the evening staff. Everyone thinks she's a stunner — and she is.

'Do you know her?' I ask Caspar, because I assume he knows every attractive girl — and has probably slept with them.

'No,' he says. 'She still has that pleasure to come.'

Staff and management are eager to engage with her; to be seen with her. It's a power she has, and I feel it myself. I may be thirty years older, but I am nervous in the presence of her beauty. It is a primal power, which exists beyond the bounds of society's ordering. Alesha doesn't need a manager's badge to get her way.

'Never seen a woman before?' asks Faith, tetchily.

'I've never seen *that* woman before!' says Caspar appreciatively.

'You men are so stupid!' says Faith.

'You wouldn't be jealous by any chance?'

'Jealous? She's just a girl!'

'Not from where I'm standing.'

Power is always a disaster for humans — our delusions of grandeur need such little encouragement. A little bit of luck here; a compliment bestowed there; a skill we possess admired by someone, or some grandiose notion nurtured in front of the mirror – and suddenly we're demanding that others handle us with almost reverential care.

'Do you know who I am?' we think or say.

And that's the danger for Alesha, I suppose. Will her small power make her or break her? Even now, I hear the first bitchy comment from the corner, and sense the storm clouds of jealousy gathering. As I bag my cauliflower cheese, I wish for her a magnet heart – a heart that transcends the small power granted her. The world is our oyster, if we have such a heart; if we keep beginners' minds – open, receptive and learning. If we refuse to hide behind our small power, and nurture a heart for all things – then truly, the world is ours. And all shall be well, and all manner of things shall be well.

But until then? I leave the store, step out into the street, joyfully breathe in the air – and then notice Manik at my side. He is not usually one to say goodbye.

'Heard of Casanova?' he asks.

'I have, yes. Interesting man.' I remember that he started life in holy orders; but as his diaries reveal, rather wandered from that path.

'"The thing is to dazzle,"' says Manik.

'Sorry?'

'"The thing is to dazzle." That's what Casanova said.'

I'm struggling a bit here, and keen to be gone. 'What – and that's your mantra?' I ask hesitantly.

Manik smiles, pats me on the back, and returns inside.

25.

WHEN THE JOKER
NEEDS A GAG

*In which Stav tells a joke, and Simon
seeks guidance from the Queen. Caspar
and Winston join in with the comedy —
which has an eternal quality. Then
Sumo arrives — and things kick off
around the fruity coleslaw.*

'Some days at work are better than others,' as Plato probably said. And for me, today was about Stav and Sumo. I will leave you to decide if it was one of the better ones.

Stav is loitering close by. This can only mean one thing – he has a joke to tell me.

'OK, Stav?' I ask.

'I suppose you better hear it,' he says.

'Ah.'

'Yes, the jokemeister cometh.'

I make every effort to look interested, as he moves forward and traps me by the oranges. Once here, he is like a priest in a pulpit – suddenly and undeservedly powerful.

'Well, the rest of the store is cracking up over this one,' he says, 'and I wouldn't want you to miss out.'

I'd love to miss out, to be honest; missing out is really underrated. 'I'd surely never recover,' I say.

'It seems to be my duty in life to amuse the troops,' he adds wearily. 'The troubadour of the aisles.'

'Mmm.'

'Oh well, keeps 'em happy, I suppose.' He wants some affirmation here, but I can't manage it. Instead, I wonder what the joke will be today. It was the one about the disabled prostitute yesterday, and he may simply have forgotten he's told me – and tell me again. I consider the etiquette of the situation, because it matters. How far into being told a joke you already know should you call time on things? When exactly should you smile, cough a little, and then let it be known that you have actually heard this comedy classic before – and if told it again, you may well die from laughter?

Or is that bad form, and something you should just never do? Take the Queen, for instance. If Stav was telling a familiar joke to our monarch, what would she do? Would she listen to the whole thing through – and then politely declare royal delight at 'the most amusing and surprising of punch lines'? Or would she dismiss him from court, with the words: 'One struggles to be amused by repeats, good sir – be on thy way, to find new material.'

Or better still, just execute him.

We do need some guidance here. But whenever it comes, it will be too late for me, because Stav is about to deliver. It may not be the one about the disabled prostitute, of course. It could be the one about the lesbians in the fish shop, which was last week's joke. He told me that one twice, and I didn't mention it – but I really don't want it a third time.

'Yeah, so how do you feel about grass stains on your knees, Si?'

'Sorry?'

I am genuinely thrown.

'Grass stains on your knees. Is it a big issue for you?'

'Er, no, not really.'

'You don't mind grass stains on your knees?'

'No.'

Where is this all going?

'So do you want to come camping with me?'

'You've lost me now.'

'It's two gays.'

'Oh, I see! Two gays. Yes, very good.'

'Just don't laugh too much on company time – or I'll get the sack. Laters!'

With the deed done, like Macbeth after murder, he moves quickly away. Stav is a deputy manager, sure. But he's also the comic, the gagmeister, the roving entertainer bringing a little light to our sad lives. He is the elusive pimpernel of comedy, now you see him, now you don't. He's there by the oranges – until he isn't, gone in a puff of laughter and guffaw. A joke about a spastic here, a gag about a paedophile there – he brings joy wherever he goes. He delivers the set piece, and then retires backstage. Let the audience applaud. They love him! 'Stav! He's *soooo* brilliant!'

And is he *soooo* abandoned?! I do sense this, not only in his bleak comedy; but also in the huge hole where self-worth should be. He is still a little boy, desperate for affirmation – and still telling gags to get it. So he is hurt and angry when the applause isn't loud enough; small abandonment echoing a larger one in his past. Sometimes he will not talk to me for days, if I'm not appreciative enough. And when he talks of his parents, it's with respect, certainly, but also with distance – as one who finds himself unable to relate to either. He is keen to honour them – because, I suspect, he can't love them. I remember him standing in the canteen, eating a sandwich. People were joking amiably about their mums and dads.

'I could not have had better parents,' he said with unwarranted solemnity – as though the only person who needed convincing was himself. 'Take them on, and you will have me to answer to!'

It was an odd remark. Who here in the canteen was thinking of taking them on? None of us knew them.

'No,' he continues. 'I regard myself as most fortunate.'

'Stav reelly loves his mum an' dad, doan ee?!'

They do say that in order to survive, the child – when given the choice of pleasing their parents or pleasing themselves – will always please their parents. They will become what the parents desire; not what they desire. This entails suppressing their true selves, and creating a phoney self to take into adulthood. Parents are the last battle for the child, however old the child is – and most will fight every other battle before fighting that one. Certainly Stav is some way from this particular war zone.

Caspar, meanwhile, is bored of putting out the milk. He has left his section to come looking for talent at the bus stop, outside the main window. Pretty office girls do sometimes wait there, all in a line, and Caspar tries to be there when they do. It's partly for his sake, but more for theirs. After all, they may not have met him yet – which must be really hard for them. When the bus stop disappoints, he wanders over towards me.

'Did you hear Stav's joke?' he asks.

'Yep.'

'Blinding, wasn't it!'

'Had its own charm.'

'Grass stains on your knees – do you want to go camping? Cracked me up – totally. He's a genius, that guy.'

Stav likes to be liked. Most people like to be liked, but he *really* does. He likes people to be pleased that it's his shift, as opposed to another manager's shift.

'I'm afraid it's my shift again,' he will say in the team briefing. It's a statement demanding a response, and Sapphy usually does the honours.

'Brillyan! Thaz war I sii!'

'You are a good man, Stav,' says Faith. 'You should do our shift more often.'

'Couldn't survive you more than three times a week, Faith! Only joking – you know you're my favourites.'

He does see himself as the people's favourite, and he's not all wrong. His need for affirmation becomes a self-fulfilling prophecy. People sense his vulnerability and look after him – only right now, it's me who needs looking after, as I notice Winston close by. Who let him off the tills? He does terrible damage on the shop floor with his shelf filling, and I'm hoping he hasn't come to help me.

'I presume you've heard,' he says.

'Heard what?'

'A man asks another man whether he minds grass stains on his knees…'

Oh no! It's the grass stains joke *again*! Is this what hell's like? But Winston's well away: '… he says – the man who asked the original question, that is – he says, would you like to come camping with me? It's a gay joke. Well, a joke about gays, to be completely accurate. One of them's gay, certainly. The one who asks – he's gay. But the one who is asked – well, he could be straight, which makes the joke funnier in a way; more predatory, and therefore more amusing for heterosexuals – unless they are religious obviously. My mother's religious, and there's no way she would find that joke funny; no way at all.'

Me and his mum should get together then, because I feel haunted by this gag. Ghosts are quite unable to sense people's unease at their presence, and this joke is the same. Like the murdered butler in the stately home, it keeps on appearing. Like the ghost of the old man drowned in the lake, it follows me around, placing its clammy hand on my shoulder and demanding I laugh. It's probably an abuse of my human rights. And here comes another – Sumo.

After Winston limped away, I returned to my apples with some delight. There may be a lot to put out, but they don't tell camp jokes, which is a definite plus. And then Sumo arrives in the store. First, I hear her voice; then I smell her scent; and finally, I see her approaching – an irritable wobbling hippo.

This particular customer hasn't always been called 'Sumo'. She started off as 'Consumer' because she only feels she exists when getting what she wants. While drugged by successful acquisition, she'll cause no particular trouble in the aisles, apart from your average rudeness. But – and it's a big, fat grunting 'but' – if she doesn't get what she wants, you know about it. So from 'Consumer' she became 'Consumo – the Great Complainer!' dazzling shop audiences everywhere with her breathless tirades of complaint. Until one day it just happened.

'Sumo's here,' said Caspar, and the name stuck.

Today, Sumo is in battle mode, and I am caught between the deli and the deep blue cheese. Caspar smiles at my predicament, safe behind the pasta.

'Where's the fruity coleslaw?' she asks.

'Have you checked round the corner?'

'Of course I've checked round the corner! It wasn't there yesterday, and it isn't there today!'

The will to live drains out of my shoes, and words do not readily come to mind. Caspar is now laughing with Garry, and both are making offensive gestures towards Sumo behind her back. But I am in front of her, and cannot respond. Perhaps if I close my eyes, she won't be there when I open them again. So I do – but she is.

'I mean, when's it coming?' she continues. 'Mmm?! What's going on? Not there yesterday, not here today! No fruity coleslaw! My God – call this a supermarket?!'

Her reactions are wonderfully disproportionate to the reality of the situation; but not to her psychic terror. In herself, she is facing a crisis. If you exist only in as much as you consume things, then when the fruity coleslaw goes, you go. You simply don't exist any more – so of course you scream and shout like a thwarted child. Everyone fears annihilation.

Meanwhile, as I try and tune out Sumo's rant, I think back to an interview I heard on the radio this morning. The presenter was talking to a financial guru about the economy, and things were getting tense in the studio.

'Does this mean we might have to…' said the presenter.

I sensed everyone in the studio tightening up, willing him to be careful; willing him not to display insensitivity to people's feelings.

'Does this mean that we might have to … well, there's no other way of putting it…'

Such hesitation and fear! What was he going to suggest? That we sacrifice our first born? Actively promote slavery? But no – it was to be worse; much worse.

'Does this mean that we might have to … well, there's no other way of putting it … tighten our belts, er, you know – spend less?'

The financial guru coughed, and mumbled something evasive. Realising his terrible error, the presenter moved quickly on. Let's have some weather, some sport, some gardening tips – anything to distract from the words just spoken. Spend less? Please, this is a family show!

As Sumo departs, still chuntering, I finally appreciate that consumer sensibilities are the new god to be tiptoed around and appeased; and that the only blasphemy today is to take the desires of the consumer in vain.

26.

THE BITTER FRUIT OF SUCCESS

In which we win a company
competition, but struggle with the
prize money. We remember a night to
forget — though Dilip and his stomach
enjoyed themselves. There is a touching
scene in the cold store; and oh — we
say goodbye to Pinocchio. It's his
final day.

Like a good day at Wimbledon, it all started with the strawberries.

'Good news, folks! We have won a company award,' says Stav at a team briefing.

'Most poorly run store, South-East Division?' asks Caspar.

'With Pinocchio as our "Outstandingly Crap Feature",' adds Garry. 'We must have walked it.'

'Strawberries,' says Stav, returning to his theme. He doesn't mind our boy-manager being slagged off, as one manager diminished is another more popular — and hopefully that other is him. He likes popularity, but needs also to take care. As ambitious politicians know, open disloyalty can come back and bite you. So he returns to the strawberries.

'Our sales of strawberries in July were second only to Brent Cross. So pretty amazing. And it's won us two hundred and fifty pounds.'

Two hundred and fifty pounds? Better than a poke in the eye with a sharp stick, and I am first out of the blocks.

'As the man who moved the strawberries to their prominent position by the entrance, I think the money's probably mine,' I say hopefully.

'I think you've had your reward, Si,' says Caspar.

'How do you mean?'

'You know – move a punnet, eat a punnet, move a punnet, eat a punnet.'

'Yeah – I saw yah!' says Sapphy, also speaking for the prosecution. ''Avin' a rii good tastin' session!'

It is true that I do pop the odd grape into my mouth as I go about my business in the produce section – but this is purely for customer advice purposes. And it is the same with the blueberries, raspberries and pineapple chunks. The strawberries I only ever taste if the box gets damaged – and well, maybe this has happened on one or two occasions.

'How the money is spent is up to you,' says Stav. 'So if you have any ideas, feed them through Si.'

And this is the start of our problems. One of the down sides of democracy is listening to people's stupid ideas – and having to say 'Good point' as they offer them. In autocracies you just have one bad idea – but in democracies, you have loads, and they all have to be taken seriously. Caspar, for instance, wants to spend it on a staff trip to his favourite doughnut parlour, after which we could all hang out in the car park – as he usually does on Fridays. This is a really good idea – if you are Caspar.

'I have no interest in either doughnuts or car parks,' says Winston.

'Yeah, it's 'ardly a nii oww!' says Sapphy. 'We should go clubbin' or summink!'

'And now I'm warming to the car park idea,' says Winston.

'It's easy to knock everything, Winston,' says Caspar. 'But what do you suggest?'

'I reckon everyone should be given ten pounds to spend as they wish,' he replies calmly.

'That's hardly very communal,' says Faith.

'Who says it has to be communal? I can't imagine anything worse than a staff outing. We work together – we're not friends.'

Organising outings is one of my least favourite activities in life. I remember as a parish priest having to organise the annual summer day-trip. We'd spend half the year wondering where to go, and end up in Littlehampton because of Donna. No one had particularly fancied Littlehampton, but Donna was set on it, and like any run-of-the-mill tyrant, got her way with threatened histrionics and the weak will of the majority.

'Littlehampton is by far the best place to go. By far! By far!'

Of course, by the time the day came, Donna had pulled out of the trip with some family commitment or medical condition, leaving the rest of us to spend half the day on a coach that smelt of sick, and the other half discovering that Littlehampton isn't geared up for rainy days. Still, at least towards tea time, wet and depressed, we were able to huddle together in the bandstand and slag off Donna – so it wasn't all bad.

Meanwhile back in the store, there emerges the idea of a meal out – on Sunday when the store closes early. It seems a good plan, but brings with it fresh disagreement. A meal, yes. But what sort? Indian? Chinese? Greek?

'Bangla!' says Mohammed, who thinks we should all try Bangladeshi cuisine.

'No fanks!' says Sapphy. 'I doan li'e all dem spices and stuff! An' I 'ate Chinese.'

'I love Chinese,' says Caspar.

'Well fine,' says Sapphy, 'but if iss Chinese, I ain't cumin'.'

'Nigerian!' says Ola, our cleaner.

'Nigerian? Where's a Nigerian restaurant?'

It transpires there isn't one – but that he just wants to hear his country of birth in the mix. I'm warming to Winston's proposal – that we just split the money and spend it as we wish – when, on the third day, a consensus appears around a bird. Nando's is a restaurant chain built around chicken – and appears to offend the least number of people. The vegetarians can at least enjoy the onion rings, which I'm told are very good.

But the evening itself is a struggle. We are a gathering of every race and religion under the sun, feeling our way towards 'a really good night out' – but with nothing in common except second prize in a strawberry contest. As Winston said, we are work colleagues, not friends, which is why he doesn't come.

And as it turns out, Sapphy never makes it either. As I hear the following day, she was actually on her way when overtaken by circumstances. 'I wazz on the bus to the restaurant, rii, when my phone went,' she says tearfully. 'It was my ex. Ee tole me vat iz noo girlfren iz pregnan'. Well, I doan li'e it, but get viss, rii – she gor pregnan' while we was still togevaa. Wor a scumbag!'

'Yep.'

'Well, sorree an all vat, but vere was no way I was cumin' to Nando's af'er I 'erd vat!'

Not that Dilip missed her, because Sapphy's absence meant more food for him. He was no longer with us, but muscled in on the event on the 'Recent Old Boy' ticket. I can still see him ignoring his heaped plate as his eyes scan the table for further free pickings. He grabs at a bowl of chips, only to discover it belongs to Mohammed.

'You disgust me,' says Mohammed, and that really set the tone for the evening.

In life, we generally get what we want at the precise moment we stop wanting it. This is certainly true of second prize in strawberry competitions. Next year, I will hide the strawberries behind the kippers – winning things is overrated.

🛒 🛒 🛒

But are relationships? Because now you find me in the cold store – wondering what Caspar wants in life.

You may remember that it was here, surrounded by the milk delivery, that I became chair of the shop union. It's not the Grand Ballroom of Versailles, but has its own chill charm, and bacon to spare. But can I save Caspar's bacon? – for it's a sad story that brings us here.

'I need to have a word,' he says, finding me by the biscuits.
'Sure.'
'Not here.'

The biscuits are usually a good place to talk, tucked away by the store's emergency exit. But apparently, it's not tucked away enough.

'We could go to the cold store,' I say.

Caspar has girlfriend troubles.

'I think I might be losing her, Si – what should I do?' I am surprised by his sadness – after all, he was hardly Mr

Commitment. Yet here he was, crying on my shoulder over a girl. 'She's suggesting we cool it for a while.' She should join us in the cold store, then; we could all cool it together.

'There's another guy who works at her place. He's hitting on her – I know he is.'

'But you still want her.'

'Of course, yeah.'

We consider the relationship for a while, and it does appear to be creaking. But then there are worse things in the world than relational creaking or collapse.

'It'll be all right, Caspar,' I say.

'No it won't – I'm losing her.'

'Lose her, find her, I know it seems hard and not the moment to say it, but, well – it will be all right in the end.'

'That's easy for you to say.'

'No, it's not,' I say, because I don't find the words easy at all. 'I've known very bleak times, believe me. I nearly jumped off a cliff once in despair, and have cried through a lot of shattered dreams. But I also know that whatever happens, it will be all right – because nothing is the end of the story. That's what I've discovered. Stories change, mine certainly has – but they don't end. And yours is a good story, Caspar, just beginning.'

🛒 🛒 🛒

Unlike Pinocchio's. For today, Pinocchio is leaving the store. He's been with us for two restless years, waiting only for his airlift out – up, up and away to higher things. He's going to a bigger store, to be a Commercial Director. But how will he say goodbye? And how shall we?

I remember my own leaving of the priesthood. The deep sadness of saying goodbye to the familiar and loved only became apparent to me in the final two weeks. On my last two Sundays, I was unable to say the blessing at the end of the service. I opened my mouth to offer the words, but nothing came out. Again and again I tried, but I could sense nothing was going to happen. After twenty years of speaking on every subject under the sun, I was finally lost for words. It didn't matter, of course, because people blessed me instead, stepping out from their seats to hug me. But as I learned, when it comes to leaving, who knows what's going to happen?

I suspect Pinocchio feels little today. He determinedly avoids the garden of sadness – and nothing looks likely to change as now he takes his leave. He engages with career and promotion, but not with people; and just as he didn't gather us together when he arrived, neither does he gather us together on this, his last day. It is as if, somewhere inside, he doesn't quite believe he exists. Instead, he flits round the store in his usual manner, while various staff huddles form, to decide what to do.

'So will you shake his hand?' asks one.

'I don't know. I might do,' says another.

'I'm not shaking his hand,' says a third.

'Nor am I! No way! Why should I shake his hand? He's a lying shit!' says a fourth.

'I'll say goodbye if he says it to me.'

'Oh yeah – well, I'll say goodbye if he says it to me. I mean you can't not – you can't not say anything.'

'You can.'

'I s'pose.'

'But I mean – I'm not seeking him out or anything.'

'I'll probably shake his hand.'

'Really?'

'Why not? I mean, there's no harm in it.'

'Well, that's up to you, mate.'

'But we're not going to clap him out of the store, like we did with Yasmin?'

'No fucking chance.'

Yasmin left last year. She was a middle-aged Muslim woman; a reliable and mature presence on the shop floor – the sort of employee any manager would want to keep. Except ours, apparently – she resigned frustrated at not being allowed to collect her children from school when circumstances left normal arrangements in tatters for a week. But hopefully she enjoyed her farewell. Mohammed organised a card and some flowers, and everything stopped as we applauded her out of the building – a thing unknown in the store. I think she was crying as she reached the door.

No two leavings are the same, of course. I remember as a priest having to move a play group on, after years of subsidising them in the church hall. We had got on famously down the years with much laughter and shared ventures – particularly the annual parish pantomime. But with the decision made, the worm turned. They ceased communication, vandalised parts of the premises, and on their final day, left rotting fish in any number of places. It was two weeks until I finally found the tuna in the piano.

But today, the only fish on the premises is fresh or frozen; and it's goodbye to Pinocchio. I stand in the produce aisle and watch the clouds through the large glass panes. I enjoy watching the clouds as they say hello and goodbye all the time; a constant coming and going, forming and dismantling in ever-changing shapes and patterns. 'Life is change, and to be perfect is to have changed often,' as Cardinal Newman said. And with that thought, I go off to find Pinocchio. He is in the warehouse, rucksack over his shoulder.

'Goodbye, Paul,' I say, as I shake his hand. 'I wish you well.'

'Thank you, Simon.'

He is vocally tight in his response, but I hope he knows it's true. I do wish him well, as he walks through the shop, looking neither to the left nor to the right, and then out into the street. He was given neither a card nor a present; but then he never gave himself.

27.

THE MONEY GIRLS, GREEN THINGS AND MOPS

In which Babs and Shazy cock up in
the office, and Winston finally cracks.
Oh dear! Hold on to your hats now,
folks! Meanwhile, Lottie carries the
company torch for all things green;
we hear the tragic story of the
yoghurt, and there's a small problem
with the wine.

The incident that became known as 'Winston and the Money Girls' occurred in a vacuum of power – which is never a good idea. When people stop believing in God, they don't believe in nothing – they believe in anything, and there is the same epistemological uncertainty now. With the loss of Pinocchio, we have a cover manager, called Leslie – and cover managers are as useful as sun cream in a storm. As with supply teachers, circumstances deny them authority – and when the centre cannot hold, mere anarchy is loosed upon the world. Anarchy, in this instance, called Winston.

But first we must meet the Money Girls – new arrivals in our story of supermarket folk. The money girls are called Babs and Shazy – and are employed as eye candy for the management team. They may occasionally look at figures on the computer screen or mishandle the petty cash. But these are secondary activities to providing a girly audience for management jokes, swinging playfully on their office chairs and running for the first aid box when Glyn scalds his hands on a Starbucks.

With Babs and Shazy, we are some way from the world of high finance – and competence.

'Oops!'

'What's up, Shazy?'

'That's not meant to happen, and so it isn't!'

'Computer playing up, is it?'

'Don't know what happened there.'

'Did it go "ping"?'

'Sort of ping, yeh.'

'Went ping yesterday.'

'I've lost the figures, I think!'

'Then it's definitely the same "ping" as I got yesterday.'

'It was the evening shift's wages.'

'I wouldn't worry.' Nothing worries Babs – as long as it doesn't affect her. She remains wonderfully untouched by the pain of others.

'It's strange, isn't it,' says Shazy, still slightly troubled, 'how one minute, the numbers are there, and then–'

'–and then the next minute, ping! – and they're gone! It's a mystery world, Shazy.'

'Gotta mind of its own, this computer!'

'Still, least said, best mended, eh?' says Babs.

Crucial to our story is one simple fact: Babs and Shazy don't like it on the shop floor. This has become apparent since their arrival. They may be paid the same as the rest of us, but there's a sense of them being separate; set apart from the common herd. Because they work close to management, they think they nearly are. They're 'office', not 'shop' – and that makes all the difference. It certainly did on this particular day.

Sometimes the money girls are kicked out of the office. Perhaps there's a confidential phone call to be made, or a disciplinary meeting. On such occasions, they pick up their make-up bags and make the canteen their office. It would be more useful if they went onto the shop floor, of course, where the tills are ringing for more staff, and the shelves need filling. But when did the money girls ever do anything useful? It's a ridiculous idea. And Winston is about to have a problem with them.

There is some previous here. As I've mentioned, Winston had once worked in the office, but was moved on, due to incompetence. This humiliation still lingers as he walks into the canteen for his coffee break – and finds Babs and Shazy sitting where he wants to sit.

'Er, excuse me, but this is a canteen, not an office,' says Winston.

'It's whatever we want it to be, Winston.'

'No – it's a canteen.'

'Get over it, Winston.'

'You do know that while you sit here gossiping, we haven't got enough people on the shop floor?'

'Oh yeah? And when does anyone help us do our job?'

Winston blinks through his thick glasses and tries to think of a clever answer.

'No, precisely,' continues Babs, 'so why should we do theirs?'

'Could I sit down, please?'

'If you like.'

'You're in my chair.'

'Then find another.'

It is at this point that something switches in Winston's brain, and a few seconds later he is out on the shop floor. 'Excuse me, everyone!' He is standing at the top of the meat aisle, and there isn't immediate hush. But my goodness, it isn't long in coming, as he strides towards the tills, his normally quiet voice transformed by rage.

'I'm sorry there aren't enough people on the tills!' he shouts. 'But Babs and Shazy are sitting on their backsides in the canteen, filing their nails! They're there now. They're "office", you see – so they imagine they're above all this; all this fucking customer nonsense!'

Winston gestures dramatically around him, to an audience that is now very hushed indeed. Leslie, the cover manager, turns a whiter shade of pale, and moves towards Winston with speed. But Winston is spent, his peaceful protest done. Like Gandhi, he allows himself to be ushered away without a struggle.

'What do you think you're doing?' hisses Leslie.

'Only saying as I find,' says Winston loudly, to his adoring public. 'Only saying as I find.'

He is guided back to the safety of the warehouse.

'Well said!' shouts Caspar from the bakery. Usually Winston's fiercest critic, he is a fan today. 'The man's a legend. That speech was right up there with Martin Luther King's "I have a dream."'

'More like "I have a moan",' I say.

But dream or moan, there is a general feeling on the shop floor that an irritating itch has just been wonderfully scratched. And the relief, like Shazy's skirts, is almost indecent.

Lottie hits the ground running, taking us all by surprise at our early morning team briefing.

'We're not green with envy,' she says. 'We're green because we believe in it!'

At 7.00 am, no one knows what they believe – it's far too early for strong convictions. But as our new 'Green Rep', Lottie has been planning her speech over the weekend, and delivers it with confidence now.

'We have to look at what we do,' she continues, 'and ask, "Why am I doing this?"'

Actually, this is a question most of us ask, most of the time – so she's pushing at something of an open door.

'I'm doing this because I can't find anything better,' says Winston.

'Right,' says Lottie, slightly thrown. Speeches prepared in front of a mirror do not cope well with interruptions. 'That may be true–'

'It is true.'

'Yes, but I'm thinking of green things.'

'Frogs?'

'Don't be a prat, Winston,' says Caspar.

'And anyway, not all frogs are green,' says Mohammed. 'Some are brown. I have seen them. And in my country, there are yellow frogs, orange–'

'Like paper,' says Lottie, trying to re-establish her authority. 'Paper is a green issue, because paper kills trees.'

'Paper doesn't kill trees,' says Winston. 'People kill trees – to make paper.'

'Same difference,' says Faith.

'The question to ask is: do you need to use all the paper you do?'

'I don't use any paper here,' says Winston. 'Apart from in the toilet.'

'Well, keep going with that,' says Garry quickly.

Green initiatives must know their limits.

As supermarkets compete to be 'greener than thou', every one of our stores now has its own 'Green Rep'. It's a good idea, and we must just hope it has more legs than the whole Disability thing, a couple of years back. In those days, it was I who was declared the new in-store 'Disability Czar'. I was sat down in front of a training video, and then told to wait for initiatives to flow from on high.

'This is a tidal surge, Si,' I was told, 'and we mean to catch it! Here begins major change, both in terms of who the company employs, and how we serve disabled customers.'

But the tidal wave passed us by. My forty-five minutes in front of the video was the sum total of the initiative, for I never heard of it again. I was a Disability Czar handicapped by lack of follow-up.

So what happens now? Well, we do our best. A blind man does come into the store occasionally, and Rosemary is onto him like a leech, parading her care and compassion – she'll do anything to get out of stacking shelves. And there is also a dwarf who shops with us, and I try to ensure I'm filling shelves somewhere near him, aware that he is unable to reach at least two thirds of the items on display.

But that's about it for the major disability initiative; a crumbling empire before even it was built.

🛒 🛒 🛒

Meanwhile, back in the canteen, Babs may sneer, but Lottie is an excellent choice for Green Rep. She's another new arrival, sure, but as a white South African who loves to travel, she brings an international perspective to the cause. She's liked – which helps – and a vegan who lives happily on grass, gravel and lettuce. Oh, and she goes on camping trips to Croatia and Sardinia, which again seems to elevate her above the rest of us.

Winston's aggression continues, however: 'How can a supermarket promote green issues when it is the single biggest promoter of waste? Here's a statistic you may not know: in Britain, 1.3 million unopened cartons of yoghurt go the way of the bin every twenty-four hours. That's 475 million unopened cartons thrown every year! Are the supermarkets proud of that?'

'Well, I'm not sure the supermarkets are to blame,' says Lottie, who probably feels they are, but now feels obliged to defend them.

'So why do they put the milk at the far end of the shop? It's not to promote sensible shopping.'

This is pretty unanswerable. How often, as I pack a customer's bag, do they say: 'And I only came in for some milk!' My record was serving a customer who only came in for some milk – and spent £73.

Before throwing it all away, obviously.

But moving on from the tragic yoghurt, I'm now attending to further waste. Someone has dropped a bottle of wine at the tills, and we have the European wine lake over our floor. There are ten ladies a-leaping, and a really angry young man whose brand-new white trainers have been baptised in Bordeaux.

'How can I wear these, mate?' he says. 'I want some compensation.'

Those whom the gods would destroy, they first make believe

that their trainers are fashion accessories. I send him off to see Leslie, while I fetch the mop and bucket and start the big clean. The mop stinks, because no one bothers to clean it after use, and soon I'm getting more complaints about the mop than the wine. And not just from the customers:

'That mop, Si,' says Sapphy from the tills – 'it smells well iffy!'

This is the trouble with institutional mops – they're everyone's and no one's. And of the two, no one tends to look after them. People look at me with increasing distaste – as if it is I who smells! *Moi?* As the Chinese sage Lao Tse probably said, 'Don't judge a man by his mop – because he who used it last week to clear up the rotten eggs should definitely have washed it afterwards. Lazy bastard.'

28

THE COMING OF KONG

In which our new manager arrives,
and staff speculate — as you do. He is
not a man to mess with, it seems.
Rosemary thinks Simon's a dream, but
does Kong think he's a Nazi? And then
an unlikely angel.

There were black clouds and thunder the day the new manager arrived. It was real Macbeth weather, full of dark portents and brooding horror. Inside the store, the colourful special offers do their best to cheer the faint-hearted, but this morning we are a neon outpost on a blasted heath of grim tarmac, lashed by grey rain. Brian, our resident witch, must be wondering where the other two are.

'I think that's him,' says Caspar, as a heavy-coated figure steps in from the cold.

'Could be,' I say.

'Or the missing link,' says Garry.

'He's large.'

We watch the figure making his sodden way through the store, to the office area. He doesn't seem to register his sur-roundings, but moves with the steady assurance of one whose path is set.

'From Pinocchio to King Kong,' says Caspar, as the figure disappears through the door.

We wander over to the tills, where in the absence of customers on this foulest of mornings, Sapphy and Faith are reading OK! magazine.

'That's him,' says Caspar.

'Ee looks a bit of a monstaar!' says Sapphy.

'At least he's a real man,' says Faith.

'He's probably gay,' says Winston wearily. 'In fact, almost certainly.'

'Gay? How would you know if he was gay?' asks Faith.

'Read the signs, my dear. Earring in left ear. Gay.'

'That doesn't mean you're gay!'

'Put it like this – it's a very strong clue.'

'I heard he was married,' says Garry.

'Well, that would be classic,' says Caspar.

'What would be classic?'

'The classic manoeuvre of a gay man who hasn't yet come out. It's the cover story. I'm married! Everyone thinks you're straight. Getting married is the surest sign of being gay.'

It is good to have sorted out the new manager's sexuality – and he hasn't even reached the office yet.

🛒 🛒 🛒

But he is hairy. As I talk with him in the office later, I see thick body hair sprouting above his collar line; and the backs of his hands are well carpeted. I find myself hiding my hairless little mitts in my pockets. As Faith said, 'A real man' – and there is certainly something of the beast about him. He's squeezed into a manager's suit and tie, but there is the feeling he could burst out any minute, and become the Incredible Hulk. I decide not to bring up the whole gay thing, and note instead the scar on his neck, and the watery eyes through which he stares. Pinocchio's eyes jumped about, this way and that – scanning, assessing and frightened. Kong's eyes just stare; deep pools staring.

'Yes, so I've chaired the shop union for a couple of years now,' I say breezily.

Kong nods slowly. He does everything slowly, and is not given to polite chat. I wonder if I'm talking too fast.

'Do you do any good?' he asks.

It's a simple question, but I'm immediately on the back foot. Do I do any good? I know it's an enquiry that may be made on Judgement Day, but I'd been hoping to avoid it until then. 'Do I do any good?' Perhaps this is judgement day – it is certainly the weather for it.

'Well, I hope we've done some good things over that time,' I say confidently, whilst trying to think of one. I can only remember the water cooler affair, which was a complete disaster. Don't mention the water cooler affair.

He smiles and says nothing. There follows a pause in the proceedings – proceedings that, in many ways, were already a pause. When a pause becomes a silence is a matter for debate, but I'm sure we were nearly there, when he spoke again.

'I've got nothing against the union,' he says.

And although it could sound like faint praise – in Kong's mouth, it sounds rather wonderful and affirming.

And later on in the canteen, he spoke with more of the staff – though it was hardly a traditional meet and greet session.

Sapphy is in full flow, having a go at squatters who are currently occupying her brother's student house.

'I mean, I'm orr for 'elpin' the 'omeless, but vey juzz walked in while ee was ow shoppin' and took over the gaffe!'

'And there is absolutely nothing the police can do,' says Brian with some relish.

'Why's that?' asks Caspar.

'Because it is a civil and not a criminal offence,' continues Brian, who clearly knows his judge from his jury. 'Section Six, Criminal Law Act, 1977.'

'Sounds criminal to me,' says Caspar, who tells me that he can imagine nothing worse than have his personal possessions become the temporary property of others. 'And dirty others, at that. No, I'm sorry, Si – I could never use them after that. Ever.'

And then Sapphy is off again: 'And ven vey stick up a no-iss, rii, in the window of my bruvver's 'ome, rii, saying vat vear now ve legal owners, rii, and vat trespassers will be per-secuted! Stray up! Vey dunnit! Wor a diabolical libber-ee!'

'He'll have to go through the courts,' says Brian, who is beginning to sound like a solicitor from Wiltshire. 'That takes two weeks minimum and costs over a thousand pounds, by which time their dog has shat all over your bedroom carpet, they've broken your TV, and your front room is Syringe City.'

'It's disgraceful,' says Faith. 'In Nigeria, they would not last five minutes. There is something wrong with this country.'

'Why don't you just go in yourself?' says Kong.

No one had noticed his arrival.

'The police can't do anything,' he continues. 'But you can. I'd go in myself.'

'What – and get your head kicked in?' asks Caspar, nervously.

Kong just smiles. He clearly doesn't envisage that scenario unfolding.

'I don't care what Winston says,' whispers Faith in my ear. 'He's not gay.'

A couple of days later, Rosemary approaches me. I have unwisely wandered into the meat aisle, and am easy game.

'We need to talk,' she says.

'About what?' I ask.

'About us.'

'What's there to talk about?'

'I'm having these dreams.'

'What dreams?'

'You know – dreams.'

I'm not a great fan of other people's dreams, but I do ask her to explain.

'OK. So I'm being led towards heaven by this figure, right?'

'Sounds nice.'

'Yes, it is.'

'What does heaven look like? I've always wanted to know.'

'We're just travelling towards it. We haven't actually got there.'

'Shame.'

'Anyway, then the figure turns round – and it's you.'

'Me? I've never led anyone towards heaven.'

'Well – that's where you're leading me, babe.'

Babe? Like recycled jelly, sponge and custard – it seems a trifle familiar. Rosemary's sudden infatuation with me is taking a sinister new direction, 'And then the figure starts crying on my shoulder, and I just hold him.'

'Ah.' I am a man in a minefield here.

'And the figure was you, Si – crying on my shoulder.'

'The figure in your *dream* was me. It wasn't actually me, obviously. I was happily asleep, a few miles away.'

I feel it is important to keep a distinction between the various realities being discussed here, otherwise who knows what I'd be doing to her tomorrow – in her dreams.

'I held you on my shoulder until you calmed down,' she says.

And then another shoulder appears on the scene. It's a bigger shoulder than mine, and belongs to Kong.

'Having a good conversation?' he asks.

I'm pleased to see him, and sense no irritation in his voice. If anything, it is playful. Rosemary winks and moves away with a little skip.

'I hear there's a bit of trouble about the Jewish paper,' Kong says to me.

'No trouble really – I'm just trying to get the distributors to stop sending it.'

'Why's that?'

'It's ridiculous the amount of copies they send – and no one buys it!'

I realise, in that instant, that Kong is Jewish – and that I am looking like some latter-day Nazi, organising a book burning. This is terrible. Rosemary, where are you? I need to cry on your shoulder.

'So it's not that you're anti-Semitic?'

'No, of course not!'

Even if 'Anti-Semite' was my middle name, I wouldn't be telling Kong. As Faith said, he is a real man, who seems to favour direct action.

'I didn't think you were,' he says with a smile.

Relief flows through my little body; like someone who has

been through the whole Nuremburg experience and been utterly vindicated.

'Good!'

'I just took a phone call about it,' says Kong, 'and I wanted to know what they were talking about. So they don't sell?'

'Not really, no.'

I was glad no longer to be considered a soulmate of Eichmann. I still, however, wanted to lay my 'I'm OK, you're OK, we're all OK' credentials very clearly on the table, so I explained more thoroughly than was usual what I was doing.

'Since I took over the magazines and newspapers – which were a complete shambles – I've been trying to rationalise the deliveries so they relate in some way to the sales. At the moment, it almost works inversely – the more we send back unsold one week, the more they send us the next. We have loads of unsold or unsellable stock taking up space in the warehouse – and it's hard convincing a computer to change its mind.'

'I'll leave it with you,' says Kong, uninterested in the detail. He had what he came for, and sloped away in his soft-soled shoes.

Pinocchio, our previous manager, had preferred hard-soled shoes – shoes which made a busy noise on the shop floor, and put staff on edge without him having to say or do anything. His shoes were his voice, in a way. Kong, however, likes soft soles – he doesn't like to announce his arrival until he's right by your side. And he certainly doesn't need his shoes to speak for him.

'He's Jewish, isn't he?' says Rosemary, catching me by the pizzas.

'I don't know. Does it matter?'

This was not a conversation I wished to have. You never quite knew how Rosemary would use information at a later date.

She had a quick and negative intelligence which stored everything – knowing all things had a use eventually. Jehovah's Witnesses had a history of remarkable bravery against the Nazis during WW2 – perhaps their finest hour – but I didn't trust her with this.

'Do you think he's a good manager?' she asks. Her golden eye shadow sparkles in the neon light.

'I like him,' I say.

Still a little disturbed, I go down towards the tills, to survey my newspaper and magazine kingdom. I love putting the newspapers out early in the morning, all crisp and even – and reading the football news as I do. There's not much I don't know about the world of sport, by 7.30 am. By the afternoon, however, the crisp papers are crisp no more – they've been worked over a bit, and soiled by life; and this is how I feel as the shift comes to an end.

'What do you call a king who's a foot tall?' asks Caspar.

'I don't know.'

'A twelve-inch ruler.'

I enjoy the joke and feel healed in some way. And things just get better and better when he then offers me a lift home in his flash car. (And no – I haven't a clue how he affords it.)

'I'm going your way today,' he says.

Sometimes, angels are conspicuous by their absence – but right now, mine is up close and personal, and looks very much like Caspar.

My limousine awaits!

29

A MOST EMBARRASSING INCIDENT

In which Babs and Shazy mislay their souls, and gang up on Lottie. A goblin appears; we witness a most embarrassing incident; face a 'morale questionnaire' and consider the truth or otherwise of the latest office rumour. And then Winston's bombshell!

Life is about souls meeting. It's very good when it happens, but doesn't happen that often – because instead of risking our soul, we usually send an impostor, to fill in. They do a decent enough job, by and large, and get us through the day. The only thing is, when the impostor gets upset, they don't refer back to the soul – they sub-contract further, and send an attack dog in their place. By the time the attack dog's let loose, we are a long way from our soul, and I only mention all this because there's some routine unpleasantness going on in the canteen.

Babs and Shazy – 'two cows who've mislaid their field' as Caspar says – have temporarily mislaid their souls, and are ganging up on Lottie. We're back with her holidays in Croatia and Sardinia – which just seem a bit too posh. Lottie defends herself against these allegations.

'We don't stay in hotels – we sleep rough sometimes.'

'Oh, you like a bit of rough do you, Lottie?' says Shazy, as we sink into a scene from *Carry on Camping*.

'Camping's too intense for me,' says Babs.

'Well, of course it's in tents,' says Caspar, filling in for Sid James.

'That's what I said.'

'No – in tents. Camping.'

'Intense, yeh.'

'Never mind.'

Babs has clearly undergone a humour bypass; and what Babs doesn't laugh at, Shazy doesn't laugh at. All for one, and one for all, with the money girl musketeers.

'Sardinia is really beautiful,' says Lottie.

'What – full of art galleries, I suppose?!' says Babs.

'Napoleon was exiled there.'

'Well, you wouldn't go there out of choice, would you?' says Babs, snorting with amusement. 'I prefer some place where you get a tan. Eh, Shazy?'

'Yeah.'

'Otherwise, what's the point?'

'I'm not that bothered about a tan,' says Lottie.

'Tell me something I don't know!' says Babs. 'You're as pale as off milk, girl. No offence.'

Lottie raises her eyebrows, clearly stung.

'You ain arf gor a gob, Babs,' says Sapphy. 'You wanna watch yoursell – Lottie's me mite!'

'Each to their own,' says Babs, 'each to their own. And anyway, Lottie, you don't have the skin for it, for the sun, do you? Be honest. You've got what I call, well, "eczema skin" – you know, goes all peely in the heat. No offence.'

'Could you stop saying "no offence"?' says Lottie, with watery eyes.

'I like a good bronzing, that's all. I'm thinking of Rhodes next year. Apparently it's like a bloody oven there.'

'Yeah, my friend went there,' says Shazy. 'Said it was fucking amazing. Not a cloud in the sky for two weeks, and didn't sober up until landing back at Heathrow.'

'Are you two joined at the hip?' asks Winston.

'Not a word that's ever going to be used about you!' says Babs.

And then a mystery voice disturbs the attack dog. 'Er – should you all be in here?'

An unknown face has appeared at the door of the canteen – and one that bears an uncanny resemblance to a goblin. Are we all appearing in an episode of *Noddy and Big Ears Go Shopping*? He must have goblin somewhere in his family tree.

'Yes, thanks,' I say. 'And you are?'

We are meant to ask strangers who they are, so it isn't a rude question. But the goblin doesn't answer – merely withdraws. We later discover that he isn't a stranger – but a new deputy manager.

'That man is one serious goblin,' says Caspar.

And really, there is nothing more to say about Gobbo, until the following day. And then there's plenty.

🛒 🛒 🛒

I am minding my own business, filling the produce section. I am enjoying the variety of colours, and counting myself the luckiest man in the world to be surrounded by such glory. Suddenly, I hear Faith scream on the tills. I look round, and see her choking with laughter. On reflection, it wasn't so much a scream as a shriek – and the reason is standing nearby. Gobbo has dropped in on the store – in his squash outfit.

The jury's still out on whether people should drop in to work on their day off looking determinedly casual. There's a case to be made for it. Perhaps you have a new shirt that you want everyone to see. You want to say, 'Hey, guys – this is the *real* me!' But no jury would have acquitted the Goblin Man.

'What does he think he looks like?' asks Faith, as Gobbo moves slowly but sportingly through the store.

'This is the most embarrassing moment in the history of the world,' says Caspar, still in shock.

Gobbo is wearing a thick gold headband, a tight short-sleeved shirt; mincing virgin trainers, and brief shorts that seemed to give access to all areas.

'Get those batty-riders!' says Caspar.

'What are batty-riders?' asks Lottie.

'Those shorts,' explains Caspar, before anyone reached for the Pocket Oxford Dictionary.

Gobbo tries to make it look like he's just dropped in on his way somewhere; that he's passing through, and eager to be away and playing hard-ball squash. But then he seems happy enough loitering in the aisles, showing off his hairy legs and moderately decent thigh muscles – for a goblin.

'Are you all right?' I ask.

'Just in to see the manager,' he says. 'Rotas to sort out.'

'That's OK then – I feared you were modelling the new staff uniform.'

'No. Just off to get some squash in. Anyway, you focus on – what's your section?'

'Produce.'

'Produce, yeah. You focus on that.'

'Right.'

He disappears backstage for a few minutes, before returning through the store and out into the street. Obviously the whole rotas thing has been put on ice.

'I'm sorry, Si, but there's no way he's going to play squash,' says Caspar. 'He just came in to give us all a look-see.'

'A look-see of what?' asks Sapphy. 'It's not like ee's Batman or anyfing, in 'is funny li'al shorts.'

'I don't think that's how he'd describe them.'

'Juzz tellin' it li'e it izz. Funny li'al shorts. What else are they?'

The most embarrassing thing I ever did as a priest was losing the coffin between church and cemetery. We had had the funeral in the church and were now to travel to a cemetery some distance away. I would normally travel in the undertaker's car, but today I took my own, as I was to travel on afterwards. No problem – I'd just follow the hearse. But the hearse was apparently driven by Lewis Hamilton, and went off at such a pace – a hearse hurtling – that we were soon separated by the busy London traffic. It wouldn't have mattered, but I had no idea which cemetery we were going to. After some miles, much sweat and with no sign of any hearse on the horizon, I turned despairingly for home. I don't know who buried that dear man in the end – but it wasn't me.

But back in-store, I am talking with Margaret and Edna, my favourite elderly sisters, as Gobbo leaves the store.

'Who was that?' asks Margaret.

'Don't laugh – but he's a new deputy manager.'

'Rather pleased with himself, I'd say. Eh, Edna?'

Gobbo's aftershave still lingers in the aisle as Edna squeezes the tomatoes. 'Reminds me of young Hobson,' she says.

'Remember him?'

'He worked in accounts for a while,' explains Margaret. 'Edna took rather a shine to him, as I remember.'

'I did not!' says Edna. 'If anything, it was you who was swooning!'

'Me? Swooning over Hobson?'

'I'm going to have to break you up, ladies. We run an upright establishment here. No lewdness allowed.'

'We'd have to go a long way to be as lewd as that man's shorts,' says Margaret, with a blushing smile.

'Fair point,' I concede. 'I think it may take some time for him to recover from this.'

How long, only time would tell. The most embarrassing incident in the history of the world is not easily forgotten. But then, a few days later, things got worse.

🛒 🛒 🛒

Never let it be said that I'm a dealer in rumour, but the current rumour is this: Gobbo touched up Babs in the office. Nothing is clear, however. Babs is saying nothing, which is a pleasant first, and the Goblin is brushing off the whole affair as a mis-understanding.

'Perhaps it's about time everyone got on with some work,' he says, on discovering us talking about him in the canteen.

But the fire of speculation is not dowsed by these words. If anything, it burns even brighter.

'I think we can take that as a "no comment",' says Winston. 'And we all know what "no comment" means.'

'Ee's a rii perve,' observes Sapphy.

Gobbo's on thin ice. First the squash clothes affair – and now this.

But we had troubles of our own that day. Head Office, in its wisdom, has seen fit to compose a 'Morale Questionnaire' and send along a MAD – Morale Advancement Delegation – to come and see us.

'These forms are about helping the company to help you,' says the MAD woman in the team briefing. 'So I'd be very grateful if you could give it your attention today, and post your answers in the Freepost envelopes provided.'

'Pay us better and treat us better,' says Caspar. 'That would help morale – you don't need a pile of forms to know that.'

'The benefit of feedback of this nature,' says MAD, 'is that it gives the company information to help target particular areas of need.'

'Like my bank account.'

'It's not just about money.'

'It is with me.'

'Well, I think there's a bigger picture – a picture that takes into account your whole experience of the workplace.'

'The fing vat gets me down…' says Sapphy.

'Yes?' says MAD expectantly.

'Izz fillin' in forms like viss. I 'ate forms!'

MAD is clearly disappointed that the morale form is bad for morale.

'I mean, no offence or nuffin',' continues Sapphy, 'but it ain't as if anyfing changes!'

'Plus ça change, plus c'est la même chose,' said Lottie, in South African French.

The MAD woman left shortly after, and I did try to sound supportive as she passed me in the produce aisle.

'Yours must be a hard job,' I say.

'People do struggle to see the value of these morale forms, yes. It's a great shame.'

A great shame? What is she talking about? My sympathy for her disappears in an instant. And how many of the forms actually made it back to Head Office, I'm not sure. I saw at least two being shredded, which is one way to deal with your anger at irritating and meaningless bureaucratic intrusion in your life. Faith also made the best of bad times, scavenging all spare Freepost envelopes.

'I just need to change the address and I can use them for my party invites.'

This was a good idea, as long as she *did* remember to change the address – otherwise she could look forward to a strong Head Office presence at her birthday bash.

But the thing is, to get back to the office rumours – I don't think Gobbo did molest Babs. He says he was just leaning over to show her something on the screen, and though that's the standard line for every office perv – I think I believe him. And so does Detective Inspector Caspar.

'For a start,' he says, 'if you were going to molest anyone, you'd molest Shazy, wouldn't you? No way would you choose Babs.'

This was a fair – if inadmissible – observation. If forced to molest someone, I too would probably opt for Shazy. But more telling still was Babs's hesitant testimony. It turned out she only said to Shazy that 'it was *like* he was touching me up.' Shazy had dutifully passed this on to the rest of us, with our imaginations filling in the blanks. But I sensed some guilt in Babs. She knew she'd indulged in some attention-seeking, and accused Gobbo beyond the evidence — but clearly couldn't now back down. So she just went quiet instead — with the unfortunate Gobbo hung out to dry.

'These things come and go,' said Kong in our weekly meeting. 'There's always someone trying it on, in my experience.'

Did he mean Gobbo or Babs? I wasn't sure and didn't seek clarification. Kong didn't discuss things; he just stated things.

And with the office scandal duly put to bed, we thought the excitement over for the day. Only it wasn't and here's why: it was Winston who had pronounced Kong gay on arrival. His theory had since been savagely discredited by other members of staff — which may explain the spring in his step now as he finds us preparing to leave.

'Interesting,' he says.

'What's interesting?'

'Kong has just left for the day, and guess what?'

'What?'

'He was met by a man!'

30.

DUSTPANS AND QUEUE-JUMPERS

In which a union meeting is hijacked,
and a queue-jumper finds himself in
hot water. Both Gobbo and Kong make
their mark, and Sapphy has good
reason to be nervous.

We are in a union meeting trying to sort out some staff issues – and all Gobbo wants to talk about is the store dustpan and brush.

'We need to talk about the dustpan brush situation,' he says in the middle of a discussion about sick pay.

'It'll have to go under "any other business",' I say.

'Well, it's a crisis,' he says, biting his lip. 'That's all I'm saying.'

'But you're saying it out of turn,' I venture. 'Because it's not what we're talking about; and it's not on the agenda either. So at best it will have to wait until AOB.'

'Someone is stealing them,' says Gobbo, ignoring me.

'Someone's stealing the store dustpan and brush?' asks Caspar incredulously. 'Like anyone would!'

With Garry, Caspar is the other staff representative here – and more open to distraction than me.

'I replaced the brush last week,' says Gobbo.

'And it's still here,' says Garry. 'I used it this morning.'

'The brush is here, sure – but the pan isn't.'

'The pan is gross,' says Caspar. 'Who'd steal the pan?'

'You can wash them, you know.'

This clearly hadn't occurred to Caspar.

'Wash a dustpan? If you're really sad, perhaps.'

'Well, maybe someone is really sad,' says Gobbo. 'Because believe you me – pans are disappearing out that door just as fast as I can buy them.'

'Strip searches as staff leave,' says Caspar. 'That's the answer. There are only so many places you can hide a brush about your person.'

'In which case I'll do Faith,' says Garry. 'I've got warm hands – and fairly pure intentions.'

Caspar and I are laughing, Kong is smiling and Gobbo is looking aggrieved.

'You may laugh, but the issue doesn't go away. Do you want me to keep replacing them or not?'

My agenda for the meeting is tottering dangerously. There is now no one discussing sick pay, and instead a rush of interest in dustpans.

'So last week the pan was here, but the brush had gone?' says Caspar.

'Correct.'

'And this week, the brush is here – but the pan has gone.'

'Correct again.'

'Have you checked around the store?' asks Kong, as my agenda crumbles completely – strong pillars falling in a cloud of distraction and trivia.

🛒 🛒 🛒

Why does this happen? How is it exactly that the most ridiculous item always ends up hogging the agenda, and exciting most interest? Is this a law written into the fabric of the universe? I remember once attending a Church of England Synod – the Church's twice-yearly parliament – and it was the same there. Changes to the world-famous Lord's Prayer were eased through in minutes and with no great concern; and then anguished days were given to determining what exactly constitutes gay sex. Is anything above the belt permitted? Is it the belt which is the divide between right and wrong? But then – how high can you wear a belt? Or perhaps more pressingly – how low? Where did Jesus stand on the positioning of the belt? Is a belt around your knees cheating? And wait a minute – what if you wear braces? Everyone had an opinion, anyway – just like this morning.

'In my last store,' says Gobbo, 'we wrote the name of the shop in indelible ink on both brush and pan.'

Rule Number One on moving job: don't talk about your last one for at least a year. It's the pastime of the insecure.

'And how did that help?' I ask.

'It's the all-important seed of doubt,' he replies. 'Were the police to raid the thief's property–'

'You got the police involved – over a dustpan?'

'The police were not involved, no – but as I say, it's the seed of doubt sown in the thief's mind. Makes them think twice before removing the pan from the premises. Because if the police *were* to come knocking, smashing their front door down in a dawn raid, then–'

'Then at least the hallway would be dust-free?'

'I think we should contact the border authorities,' says Garry. 'Whoever's got our dustpan is bound to be making for the continent.'

'Where they'll "clean up", no doubt,' says Caspar.

'Well, now we've got that joke out of our system, I think we should come to a decision,' I say.

'Buy a new set,' says Kong decisively, 'and we'll speak about the business at the team briefing.'

'Good idea,' says Garry. 'A new pan and brush, and we start again.'

'Agreed?' I ask.

'I'm happy with that,' says Gobbo. 'It's a start at least.'

'Good. Then we'll move on.'

'It's certainly an issue which required attention,' says Gobbo needlessly.

'Well, we've given it attention,' I say.

'We don't brush things under the carpet in this store,' says Garry.

'Getting back to the sick pay...'

🛒 🛒 🛒

Meanwhile, things are kicking off at the till. Someone has been accused of queue-jumping – and queue-jumping is perhaps the worst thing you can do in England. The English conquered the world in order to teach others the art of queuing, and even if Johnny Foreigner has been a bit slow to learn, it's important that high standards are maintained at home. A scrawny man with freckles and shaved ginger hair – too twitchy and drugged for his own good – has pushed ahead of a woman who was looking at the magazines while waiting.

'Tough, madam, tough!' taunts Scrawny, as the woman tries to reclaim her position ahead of him.

'I was just looking at the magazines, you ridiculous man,' she says.

'Oh ridiculous, am I? Well, I'm ahead of you, you knob-jockey!'

'I beg your pardon!'

'I fink she waz in the queue before you, mite,' says Sapphy from behind the till, scorn oozing from her eyes.

Scrawny's unprintable reply does not go down well.

'Well, I ain't servin' you – nevaar! – and vat's a fact!' says Sapphy.

And neither, it seems, is anyone else serving him. Sapphy's scorn becomes communal amongst those on the tills, and all withdraw their labour. Better an estate agent than a queue-jumper.

'Can I help?' says Kong, who has appeared at Scrawny's side.

'This man pushed ahead of me!' says the woman.

'I'm just trying to get served, mate. Just trying to get served. Looks like you've got staff problems 'ere.'

'Ee's a fuckin' queue-jumper,' says Sapphy. 'No one's goin' to serve 'im.'

Kong looks through Sapphy, and then turns his gaze on the man. Outside the store, he would knock this punk to the ground. But what will he do in-store? 'I'm going to open a till and serve you myself,' he says, leaving Scrawny as chuffed as a peacock in June – and everyone else looking daggers.

Sapphy's dropped jaw says it all. 'Well, doan evar fink I'm goin' to serve yah!' says Sapphy.

'Don't need you, gobby! I'm bein' looked after!'

But in this instance, Kong speaks with forked tongue. He will serve Scrawny, but first, and in no particular hurry, he has to go back to the office to fetch his till key, leaving the queue-jumper high, dry and friendless by the tills. On his return, Kong then takes an age to open it, and whilst serving him, holds up some of Scrawny's fish fingers, and asks a member of staff to check the price.

'Don't want to overcharge you,' says Kong to Scrawny, while he endures a further wait. Had he kept his original place in the queue, he'd have been away twenty minutes ago – but his impatience has brought him down, as our compulsions tend to. Scrawny goes from peacock pleasure to rhino rage – but what exactly are his choices? He's not taking on Kong; and he wants his food.

'It's good to respect the queue,' says Kong as Scrawny finally leaves – drugged, twitchy and furious.

'I want to see you in the office,' says Kong to Sapphy.

🛒 🛒 🛒

And getting back to the dustpan and brush crisis, it turned out that neither of them had been stolen. Interpol could stand down from red alert, and the border authorities relax – Gobbo had got it wrong.

Faith turned out to be the culprit, hoarding them down by bakery.

'I may still need to search you,' says Garry.

'Keep away!'

'Don't worry – I'll warm my hands,' he says, blowing on them. He grabs her playfully, and she squirms free. 'So – squirrelling them away down here, eh?'

'I'm not squirrelling them anywhere – I need them. And the cleaning cupboard is miles away.'

'This will be a serious disappointment for Gobbo.'

'It's the bakery which needs them the most,' continues Faith. 'So when they appear in the cleaning cupboard, I just bring them down here. This is the cleaning cupboard now.'

It makes a sort of sense, because unlike the rest of the store, the bakery does need constant attention. It's amazing how much mess a few crumbly croissants or pains au chocolat can leave on the floor. France must get through dustpans like nobody's business.

And Gobbo? Gobbo was shaken – but not stirred, and still went ahead with his plan to buy another dustpan and brush, and write the store's name all over them in indelible ink. Kong has made his mark already, whilst Gobbo is definitely a man still trying. Though perhaps the greatest leave behind them no mark at all – just a space; a space in which others can run, jump and laugh in the freedom of it all.

Kong did not keep Sapphy long in the office, later in the day. I attended as her representative, but could do little to calm her. She was nervous, and had a right to be. Swearing on the shop floor is not acceptable, and Kong cut straight to the chase:

'If you use that language on the tills again, you will be out,' he says, before anyone can sit down.

'You din 'ear wha' ee called me!' says Sapphy.

'What did he call you?'

Sapphy tells him, and Kong looks through her with his watery stare – while somewhere inside a decision is made.

'If he returns, tell me,' he says.

'Wat yer goin' ter do?'

'He's now banned from the store.'

'Oh, rii!' Sapphy likes this.

'But as I say, if you use that language again – you're out.'

I like the cut of his jib. He's a savage – but a noble one.

31.

CLOSING TIME

Staff leave at the end of the day, and
Napoleon's career choice is questioned.
Both Christmas Past and the
Moroccans are remembered as Manik,
Sonny and Simon close the store. It's
time for farewells and bed — with just
a small diversion on the way home.

Lockers are being emptied by the evening staff. It's time to go home, for the day is done. As they signed in at 3.00 pm, so now they sign out at 10.00 pm – another day's money earned; another day's money to spend. But is it life?

'This isn't life, Si,' Ayub once told me, as he stood in the produce aisle, avoiding work – 'It's just a means to life. That's what you have to understand.'

Most of them change into their own clothes before leaving, because they have an image to maintain. I walk home in mine, because the world doesn't look at old men; and old men are not bothered if they do.

'I'd rather be dead in the street, than uniformed,' says Nathaniel.

The boys look sharp in their own urban clothes, but it's the girls who are particularly transformed. Like a butterfly from the chrysalis, the black and shapeless is discarded for the pink, gold and glittery.

'That top is *sooo* gorgeous, Izzy!'

The day is forgotten already, and they leave laughing and moaning. Boys adjust iPods in their ears, and pull their collars up as they step out into the chill night air.

'How d'you pull a fat bird?' asks Nathaniel, as they stand together out in the high street, normal people once again. 'It's a piece of cake!'

The boys laugh louder than the girls.

'*L'Angleterre est une nation de boutiquiers!*' Yes, it was Napoleon who called England a nation of shopkeepers, stealing the line from Adam Smith. In the Frenchman's mouth, it was an insult to a country he had failed to conquer, implying a race of the small-minded and petty. But, really, there are worse things to be famous for than running a shop; for opening when you say you will, and delivering as best you can the things people either need or desire. It certainly beats leading your nation's army to destruction in the Russian winter. Of the 600,000 French troops that reached Moscow under Napoleon's leadership in 1812, only 30,000 returned to tell the tale. No doubt the families of the disappeared wished Napoleon had taken up shopkeeping at an early age, and stuck with it.

Meanwhile, out in the high street, Izzy has a joke. 'There's this really weedy bloke, right? He's at a singles bar, and goes up to this girl and says, "If you can guess my weight, I'll spend the night with you." She looks at him, like he's nothing, and says, all dismissive, "Three tons." "Close enough," he says.'

The girls laugh louder at this one, as the boys feel the shame. Of course none of those leaving now will stick with shopkeeping. This is not their idea of happiness. As Sapphy says to me at least once a day: 'I juzz wanna be 'appy, Si! And this job ain't nevaar goin' to make me that! Fuckin' 'ell!'

But then supermarkets will never make anyone happy – and neither should we insist they do. We might as well ask a fish to do our typing, for the supermarket merely becomes what we are. If we bring happiness to it, then it becomes happiness. If we bring despair to it, then it becomes despair. We project our inner selves onto our experiences, and retail is no different. If our being is angry, frustrated or calculating, so will be our experience of shopping. When I was twenty, I worked for two years in another supermarket. I was Price Controls Officer there, though the name flatters me a little. I didn't control the prices – I just had to know them all, and correct any that were wrong. I wasn't ready to be happy then, however, and longed only to be out of the door. Perhaps this showed in my face, because I remember one customer who was forever saying: 'Don't worry, chuck – it might never happen!'

But I am ready to be happy now. Thirty years on, I am finally ready to be happy. For where else could I have such adventures? Whilst here, I have been a greengrocer looking after the produce section – in daily awe at the wonderful colours; I have been a newsagent – responsible for all the newspapers and magazines; and I have been a baker of crumbly croissants, spanking apple turnovers, more-ish muffins and much else beside. I have lived life, funny and infuriating, behind the tills; been responsible for reporting on attractive women at the bus stop, and chaired the shop union – representing individuals from every imaginable background, and some that were not. People have cried on my shoulder and I on theirs – but more than crying, we have laughed. With staff and customers and at staff and customers – we have laughed. There's a lot more comedy at the bottom than the top.

So really, could anyone have had a better life than me over the past few years? It's hard to imagine.

But as I say, it's time to go. The evening crew are splitting up and catching their various buses home. They'll try and blag it with old bus passes or hard luck stories and big sad eyes, but will probably have to pay in the end. Back in the store, the aisles are quiet, the tills empty and the fever of life hushed. As the shop was opened sixteen hours ago, all fresh with expectation, so Manik, Sonny the security guard and myself now close it, weary with selling. I switch off the lights in the canteen, while Manik and Sonny lock the Money Room. No one is allowed in there alone, and it's reassuring to know that burglars have tended to stick to this rule as well, always working as a team.

I take the lift up to the warehouse, which is particularly still tonight. It's a holding place for deliveries, and, tucked away from the thrust of life, has always held me too.

It's time to go, I know, but here in this place, the ghost of Christmas Past is suddenly at my shoulder, and I'm remembering — remembering the annual game of Christmas poker played out between customer and store. With sell-by dates in mind, the customer wants to purchase everything last minute. The store, on the other hand, is wary of being left with 1,000 turkeys and 478 Christmas puddings on Boxing Day. The customer wants to wait until Christmas Eve. The store wants it all done and dusted by the twenty-third. So who will blink first? The store is not going to risk a fresh delivery on Christmas Eve. Or will they?

'Will there be a delivery tomorrow?' asks a customer.

'I wouldn't bank on it.'

You have to protect yourself in these circumstances. Disappointed Christmas customers are the most dangerous.

'You mean there might be?'

'Might be, might not be. I just wouldn't bank on it.'

'If there was a delivery, when would be the best time to come? Eight am? Nine am?'

'If there was a delivery, probably around nine am. But it's far from certain.'

'You're talking like there will be.'

'I'm talking like I don't know – which I don't.'

'Percentage-wise – what's the chance?'

'You must make up your own mind; there's nothing more I can sensibly say.' This would be a good epitaph on my grave – 'There's nothing more I can sensibly say' – and there are times over the Christmas siege when the grave is not unattractive. I watch the customer put the turkey in her basket, then take it out, then put it in, then take it out – in, out, in, out, shake it all about.

'I'll take it!' she says finally.

Phew!

And when it all got too much, I'd quietly leave the madding crowd, and take myself to the solitude of the warehouse. It would be a good place for the Christmas manger, for, like all stillness, it stores so much possibility; so much to be unpacked, displayed, enjoyed. Downstairs, tempers go 'Pop!' and the tills go 'Kerching!' While away in a warehouse, I experience a peace that passes all understanding.

🛒 🛒 🛒

'Are you coming or what?!'

Manik's calling up. I check the back door, set the warehouse alarm; breathe in eternity, turn out the lights and take the lift down, where Manik is pacing the floor.

'Let's be out of here then,' he says.

And my best moment in the store today? Probably the

Moroccans; no, definitely the Moroccans. They grow our tenderstem broccoli, and with other growers from around the world, came to see what happened to their produce once it left them. So we had plum growers from Argentina, fine bean farmers from Kenya; sweet pepper providers from Spain; mango maestros from Costa Rica; grape growers from South Africa, strawberry kings from Egypt; lemon men from Israel and asparagus purveyors from Peru.

Iqbal, the more talkative of the Moroccans, was thrilled to see his creation in the western marketplace. When a customer picked up one of his tenderstem and put it her basket, he leapt in delight, and spoke excitedly to his colleague. And as I stood with Iqbal, something distant and ancient stirred in me, and I was taken back to days of yore, when we knew who grew our carrots because they lived in the same village – and worked the field down the road. Today, in the global village, the man who grows our carrots doesn't live next door, but on the next continent; and supermarkets invite us to relate to countries not fields.

This all has its own sense of wonder. Globalisation expresses ultimate truth in the oneness of all things – a truth which national borders deny. We are one before we are many. But it can also make us strangers to our food, and put distance between us and our meal. I become food-stupid, imagining shoals of fish fingers in the Atlantic, lasagne groves in Tuscany and freshly picked cans of baked beans drying in the Mexican sun. And maybe this is why it is quite such a delight to meet our friends from Morocco. I now know who grows my broccoli. It is Iqbal, and his quiet colleague, who never did tell me his name – but smiled a lot.

Meanwhile, amid the low hum of the freezers, Sonny, Manik and myself pull down the blinds on the chiller cabinets. I pick up some litter as I go. It bothers me more because it's in the produce section.

'Don't worry about the litter,' says Manik. 'It'll give the cleaner something to do tomorrow.'

'A good day, Sonny?' I ask, as he double locks the front door.

'A good day,' our security guard replies with an enigmatic smile. I have no idea whether it was good for Sonny or not, and I'm not sure he does either. Most people have to drink two pints to achieve his smiling but slightly vague grasp on reality.

'It'll be a good day when Sonny catches a thief!' says Manik.

Sonny again smiles enigmatically, and takes his leave. He's given up on the buses and brings his car now.

The camera watches as Manik sets the alarm, closes the back door and sets off with me down the street. It will take Manik an hour to get home, and then, he tells me, he'll watch some mindless TV to unwind.

'The more mindless the better,' he says. He'll need to set his alarm, however, and be back in his car by 5.30 am – because he's on an 'early' tomorrow. 'Hardly worth me leaving!' he says.

'Oh, it's always worth you leaving,' I say. 'Otherwise how can you start again, all fresh like the morning dew?'

'You're mad.'

I say good night to him by his car, and start the walk up the hill towards home. Ten minutes or so, and I'll be pushing open my front door. I stop off at an all-night Budgetmart to get some milk and bread, because the good thing about Budgetmart is that it's always open – even if it does smell of old socks. But then bed, for I too will be back tomorrow. We'll all be back – Faith, Caspar, Brian, Winston, Garry, Rosemary, Toad, Lottie, Mohammed, Manik *et al* – the whole glorious cast. We'll get up tomorrow, and do it all over again. As Beckett said, we shall try again. Fail again. Fail better.

Vive les boutiquiers!